Mind

and

Time

and

God

(an exploration in eidetic hodology)

Mind and Time and God

(an exploration in eidetic hodology)

By J. Martin Strangeweather

Cover art by J. Martin Strangeweather

Cover design by Dustin Myers

Printed in the United States of America

Published by the Santa Ana Literary Association

ISBN: 979-8-218-38610-8

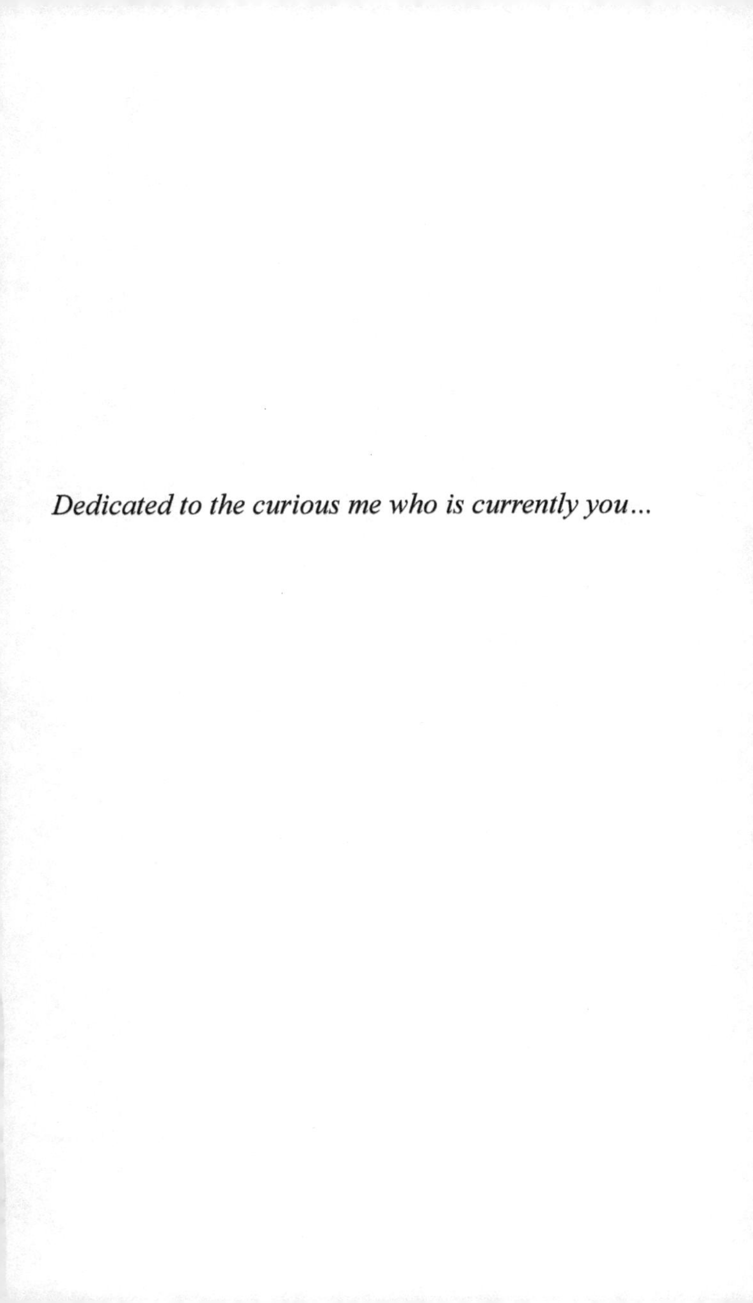

Dedicated to the curious me who is currently you…

[1]

noun, adjective: eidetic

1. A distinctive expression of the cognitive or intellectual character of a culture or social group.
2. Pertaining to or denoting mental images having unusual vividness and detail, as if actually visible.
3. An illusion or hallucination so realistic it fools one's senses and intellect. Unless noted otherwise, all instances of the term *eidetic* within *Mind and Time and God* are referring to this particular usage, even though many of the alternate definitions may also apply.
4. The outward appearance of a deity. *(according to Homer)*
5. Mere image or shape. *(according to Democritus)*
6. Truth made manifest. *(according to Parmenides)*
7. A timeless and unchanging idea with concrete substance. *(according to Plato)*

8. The invariable and essential structure/nature of an object. *(according to Edmund Husserl)*

9. Pertaining to a mode of interpretation in which matter and mind are understood to be ultimately indistinguishable. *(according to Thoth de Miurgé)*

10. Pertaining to a belief that the mind of every being on Earth (and possibly every being in the universe/multiverse) is part of a unitary whole which is itself conscious; i.e., all minds considered collectively are a singular type of consciousness unto itself, in the manner of a superorganism. *(according to Sophia Mercury)*

[2]

eidetic hodology: for the purposes of this exploration, we shall define *eidetic* as having the quality of an illusion that seems so real it is often mistaken for reality, and *hodology* is the study of pathways; therefore, eidetic hodology is the exploration of pathways that seem so real we often mistake them for reality.

[3]

How could a subatomic particle—for the sake of convenience let us describe it as a spherical object—be rotating to the left and rotating to the right *at the same time?* Answer: Look at its reflection in a mirror. In a similar vein, how could a subatomic particle be spinning up and spinning down *at the same time?* Answer: You can *A)* look at its reflection in a mirror, *B)* move the position of the observer from one side of the particle to the other, or *C)* place the spinning particle between two observers; one observer will experience it spinning upward, and the other observer will experience it spinning downward. Superpositional outcomes have nothing to do with a particle undergoing physical changes, such as branching into multiple copies of itself. It is the observer's mind which undergoes the change. Ponder this. There's only one mind, and it's everywhere all at once, but we can only experience it in a linear manner. The mind isn't bound by the speed of light and three-dimensional spatial considerations. The mind is a field—a wave *and* a particle, a sphere of awareness/influence.

[4]

The human mind is a transtemporal field of awareness, transtemporal in the sense that a human mind has the power to intentionally reexperience/recreate the past (in the form of memories) as well as project/predict hypothetical experiences regarding the future.

[5]

The transtemporal field of awareness we call *mind* extends as far as all of human experience, but individual humans may only partake in the tiny portion they happen to experience for themselves.

[6]

Ultimately we all share the same transtemporal field of awareness. We all partake from the same well, so we should strive not to poison it any further.

[7]

We can only unlock conscious experience through objects (and our imaginative abstraction of them), which confines us to experiencing consciousness in a linear manner.

[8]

Individual brains evolve individualized channels, tuning receptors, forming particularized lock combinations to store or activate certain angles of experience. Consciousness is the skeleton key that accesses them all. An object/particle/consciousness in a state of superposition adds up to more than the sum total of its various trajectories/branches. Such an object/particle/consciousness has additional properties, epiphenomenal properties, that differ from the observable trajectories of classical physics. One context seems deterministic, the other context seems random. But there is another context, a third way of understanding/perceiving reality, beyond the shortsighted perceptions of chaos and order, one which we fail to take into account altogether. Fractals are both chaotic and orderly, depending on the scale at which one encounters them, or the skill one has at deciphering patterns.

[9]

It is presumptuous to think there is a "real" world hiding beyond our theories and measuring devices, our comprehensions. Ultimately, we have only our observations. Why should we expect there is such a state as *the complete understanding of everything,* or even *the complete understanding of any single thing?* Maybe the problem (certainly a portion of it) lies within the archaic wording (and attendant archaic definitions) one must resort to in order to express concepts such as *mind, consciousness, time, reality...* What is stable? Our body is constantly succumbing to entropic forces, our mind is constantly jumping from this to that, and our perceptions are constantly pouring data into our memory bank. But it would be unhelpful to say reality is unstable, for this very instability provides the conduit for our feeling of stability!

[10]
Our standard theories of reality and the mind do not, indeed cannot, provide a complete and accurate description of the subjects they intend to describe. Why does reality seem to behave according to one framework of interaction (classical physics) for large-scale phenomena, and an altogether different framework of interaction (quantum mechanics) for small-scale phenomena? Why does reality seem to behave one way when nobody is paying attention to

it, and a different way when someone is observing it, as quantum measurements seem to indicate?

The observational transformations of the collapsing (or branching, depending on your understanding of the mechanics involved) of the quantum wave function are instantaneous, happening faster than the speed of light/perception/thought. The collapsing/branching is completely undetectable by standard measuring procedures. What mechanisms must already be in place for this to occur? Must there already be infinite variations of selves/universes at work, or are alternate outcomes manufactured right there on the spot? How else might we understand this process? Heisenberg doubted that the wave function represents a course of physical events in time and space, believing it only yields data regarding our *knowledge* of such events, whereas Schrodinger understood the wave function as representing *real, causal events*. How might they *both* be correct? A system (any object or thing, including a "mind") in a state of superposition possesses additional properties than it would otherwise. Once a particular value or outcome for the wave function is determined/allotted, the resulting state is irreversible and will determine the entire future trajectory of that particular world/consciousness. But how are the different states parceled and pared down to the one you are currently experiencing? They aren't. You are experiencing all of them simultaneously, except in this particular world/consciousness you are experiencing this particular state. Liken it to the Anthropic Principle.

[11]

The universe (i.e., the universal wave function [Hugh Everett's term for it], the all-mind, the over-mind, the mind field, the eidetic substratum [Thoth de Miurgé's term for it], the universal mind lattice [Alex Gray's term for it], Indra's jeweled net, God, reality, etc.) (each of these terms possesses their own nuanced particularities and explanatory shortcomings) in an unagitated state tends toward indecisiveness (as do our minds, because fractals repeat/reflect themselves at greater and lesser scales). It only crystalizes into various particular states when agitated, i.e., forced to meet an observing system's expectations of perception and/or measurement. The indeterminate state is commonly referred to as a superposition. For the purposes of our discussion we shall refer to the indeterminate/indeterminable state as a superposition, and refer to a superposition composed of other superpositions as an omniposition, since this term conveys a meaning/concept that is somewhat different from its predecessor. It isn't that the eidetic substratum is in one or another determinate state, but we just don't know which. The eidetic substratum is actually in every possible state: of being in a particular state and not being in a particular state, which means it has the property in question, it does not have the property in question, it both has and does not have the property in question, and neither does it have nor not have the property in question. None of the resulting states are more or less real than the others, and all of them are experienced equally, except each particular state of the observing system only experiences a fraction of the overall collapsing/branching experience. Recap: the eidetic substratum in its unagitated state is simultaneously in a state of exclusively A, a state of exclusively B, a state consisting of both A and B, and a state of being neither A nor B. This hyperpositional state is known as a superposition, and we shall henceforth refer to a superposition of superpositions as an omniposition. Omnipositions and superpositions do not consist of a multiplicity of states embedded within/layered one atop (or next to) another like the densely packed skins of an onion. The terms refer to a bound multiplicity of states which are hyperspatially interwoven, and the total field in which all omnipositions/superpositions occur is called the eidetic substratum, or consciousness/mind/reality.

[12]

The eidetic substratum appears to evolve before our consciousness in two distinct ways: through the continuous linear changes that occur due to temporal movement/displacement/decay of physical particles/waves, and the nonlinear/discontinuous/instantaneous/random shifts that occur due to measurement/observation/agitation of omnipositional states. In an unagitated/unobserved state, the eidetic substratum may be thought of as a cloudy blur of indistinct hyperstates. Since we cannot observe events at the atomic level, there's scientific reason to think such "fabrics" of the eidetic substratum are *normally* in an omnipositional blur. Even more disturbing, because we cannot observe events at the macrocosmic level, there's also scientific reason to think such events are *normally* in an omnipositional cloud of blurred hyperstates, each of which is the total history of a universe. The eidetic substratum is infinitely dense (the word *infinitely* here means *immeasurably*), has infinite mass (the word *infinite* here is meant to convey a sense of boundless expansion), and is infinite in extent (the word *infinite* here means literally *all there is and was and ever will be*). Of course, all this talk of superpositions and omnipositions and hyperstates is merely happening in one hodological network among the infinite trajectories/possibilities of the eidetic substratum.

And what is the eidetic substratum? We are the eidetic substratum. We are the eidos from which all eidetics arise.

The Big Bang itself is evidence that something beyond our current comprehension/interpretation of the "universe" must in fact exist, for the Big Bang had to spring from somewhere/something. Every direction of understanding ultimately arrives at the doorstep to the infinite mazework of eidetic hodology. Herein lies the quantum of reality, which is altogether different from discovering the formula/equation for solving/predicting/controlling the grand mystery of being/existence, and unless one understands the difference, one will miss the point of this work entirely.

[13]

Everything is information.

Everything is mind.

Your brain is processing information.

Your brain is processing mind.

Focus on a chair.

Any chair will suffice.

The chair is not outside your mind.

The chair is not inside your mind.

The chair is your mind.

Now focus on love.

Focus on divinity.

Any divinity will suffice.

These words are not in your mind right now—they *are* your mind right now.

[14]

Neuroscience seeks to explain the mental by means of a thorough description of the physical, but what if extra-physical factors (i.e., faster-than-light travel, quantum entanglement, superpositions, the collapsing/branching of the wave function) are necessarily involved in the explanation of a mind?

[15]

There is no (discernible/measurable) spatial or temporal boundary between the observer, the measuring device used for observation, and the system being observed. The observer, the measuring device, and the system under observation are quantumly entangled.

[16]

Precisely when does the collapsing/branching dynamic of a particular measurement occur? The collapsing/branching dynamic of a particular measurement has always been in occurrence, and will continue to always occur. Consciousness is much more than what you experience. Consciousness is infinitely vast, spanning infinite worlds and their worldly reflections.

[17]

The universe behaves a certain way when no one is watching, and an altogether different way under observation. Unobserved, the universe evolves in a linear, causal manner. During quantum-level measurements, however, our experience of the universe appears to jump/transform in a nonlinear, acausal manner. What is it about the observer/observation that effects such a radical change in the system's behavior? The answer could only be *consciousness* (of a very specific type/mode).

[18]

The observer is that part/mode of the system/universe/omniverse which is observing/ measuring itself; therefore, it makes no difference if the observer is human or mechanical or otherwise—it does not matter if the observer has a "consciousness" in the ordinary/everyday/human sense. An observer is simply defined here as anything that can perform a measurement and record the result.

Observers are not uniquely special (or especially divine) features of the universe, just as your eyes, ears, and nose are not uniquely special (or especially divine) features of your body.

[19]

Seen through otherworldly eyes,

Each human spreads across the hypergrid

Like a cloud of broken mirrors,

Comingling and dissipating,

Condensing and evaporating.

[20]

There is a mode of being which allows for the (seemingly*) volitional manipulation of certain expressions of the eidetic substratum. Humans are an example of such a mode of being. The mode of being could in and of itself be likened to a being, the being through which all being/volition emanates, i.e., God.

*This parenthetical cannot be stressed enough.

[21]

Sometimes our experience informs the observation, and sometimes the observation informs our experience. Every possible facet of an observer (in the quantum mechanical sense) obtains every possible observation/measurement (in the quantum superpositional sense), leaving the observer to match/record the outcome befitting their particular worldline's trajectory. Quantum probabilities have less to do with particle position/momentum and more to do with which mind/world an observer happens to occupy after a measurement/observation.

[22]

The eidetic substratum is in a perpetual state of superpositional entanglement. Quantum "jumps" from one stable worldline/position/status to another are an illusion of the observer's fragmented/ subjective perspective/consciousness. Seemingly random quantum "shifts" only occur within the relativistic experience of the observer.

[23]

There is no absolute state for any given subsystem of a superpositional system. There is only the state of the subsystem relative to the remainder of the superposition; that is, the state of any given superpositional subsystem is relative to every other subsystem state comprising the superposition; which is to say, the outcome/experience of any given quantum measurement is relative to the remaining possible outcomes/experiences in the entangled superposition. This would hold true for macroscopic entanglements as well.

[24]

One may be tempted to think physical states evolve in a linear/determinate manner, and mental states evolve in a nonlinear/stochastic manner; however, there is no distinction between mental and physical states in the eidetic substratum. Only memory records are significant, whether they arise from configurations of neurons, circuits, magnetic tape reels, or less tangible sources.

[25]

There are no absolute/determinate physical states; therefore, there can be no absolute/determinate mental states, but there can be absolute/determinate records of measurements/observations.

[26]

Just before the observer is about to open the lid of Schrodinger's box, the observer's mind is switching back and forth between expectations of a dead cat and expectations of a living cat. Indeed, the two expectations are superimposed. The observer's mind is in an entangled state of superposition. Minds think/imagine/remember via superpositions. Minds are currents/fields of superpositional awareness which allow certain physical observation systems to experience various observations without necessarily being in the attendant physical state.

[27]

What accounts for our particular experience of any given quantum measurement/observation (experiencing one determinate facet/disposition of the superposition as opposed to another) must be likened to the Anthropic Principal. In any observation involving a superposition, you experience A separately, you experience B separately, and you experience A and B simultaneously in a manner that is neither the experience of A nor B. This is the eidetic nature of reality.*

Note: There may be many more observational standpoints/states than A or B (perhaps infinitely more) for any given superpositional current of the eidetic sea.

*This cannot be stressed enough—whichever version

of the measurement/observation you experience is not the privileged or *real* one, though it's certainly not irrational for you to consider it the most important one.

[28]

Perform a quantum measurement. The result is A (more precisely, you experience the result A). Repeat the exact same quantum measurement. The result is B, yet you perceive the result as being identical to the first measurement (realize, you don't perceive the second result as A—you perceive the second measurement as if the first result were B). Repeat the same quantum measurement a third time. The result is A, and yet you perceive the result as being identical to the prior two measurements (as if they were A all along). This is because (in the entangled superpositional currents of the eidetic substratum) the result of your measurement has always been A, just as the result of your measurement has always been B.

Must reality be ultimately translatable/reducible to human intelligibility?

Eidetic hodology tends to concern itself with the limits of human understanding, and whether these limits are insurmountable or merely intractable given our current level of evolutionary/mental/technological sophistication.

[29]

From subatomic particles to entire universes, any given system tends toward a state of entanglement/superposition. Size and complexity have no bearing upon such hyperdimensional dynamics, just as size and complexity have no bearing upon that which a mirror reflects. The mirror reflects all, though the eye only catches its own reflection.

[30]

There is only one mind, of which we partake. The mind is a singularity that gathers information and expresses itself through a multiplicity of subjective physical observers, just as every single physical observer is comprised of multiple relativistic experiential states, just as every single ommatidium forms the compound eye. We are the cosmic ommatidia.

[31]

The complete description/interpretation of any given physical system will inevitably involve the concept of a nonphysical system (for example, superpositional dynamics, or the deity of your choosing).

[32]

The mind does not undergo superposition—the mind *is* superposition, and our brains have evolved specific ways of filtering/editing/tuning out contradictory sense data in order to create determinate experience. It's not difficult to imagine why having linear/determinate experiences (rather than nonlinear/indeterminate experiences) would be beneficial to the survival of a three-dimensional observer with mortal (fourth-dimensional) needs/concerns.

[33]

When we speak of multiple universes/worlds/minds, we are not in fact discussing multiple universes/worlds/minds—we are discussing quantum measurements/observations/behaviors as they appear to human observers, interpreting the multifarious probabilities/predictions of quantum mechanics in terms of our own subjective experience.

[34]

The quantum measurement problem is an inability to account for our determinate experience of indeterminate/omnideterminate quantum physical processes. What if mental states can only be experienced as determinate; i.e., what if physical (superpositional) states can only be translated into mental states as determinate experiences (single substates/dispositions of the superposition)? While reality (the eidetic substratum) is ill-defined, mind confers a continuum of determinate experiential states, ceaselessly filling in the blanks and connecting the dots, filtering out contradictory/incoherent data. Think of mind as the radio dial, tuning certain frequencies of experience in as it tunes other frequencies of experience out. The fullest description of the universe thus requires a description of the mental states/substates of the system observing it.

[35]

To explain the universe, one must inevitably explain the mind, and in doing so, the mind may be explained away entirely, merging universe and mind into one which is neither.

[36]

The superpositional trajectory/evolution of any particular mental state depends on the superpositional trajectory/evolution of every other mental state in the superposition. Mind is composed of infinite observers, with each observer continuously dissolving into an infinity of minds.* Consider how two parallel reflective planes create the illusory effect of an infinity mirror, except in this case each reflection appears slightly different and behaves independently from one another!

*In a similar vein, history is composed of endless accounts, with each account mirroring countless histories.

[37]

Does belief make the observational experience determinate, or does the observational experience make belief determinate? The answer to this question is a superposition.

[38]

Eidetic hodology is the study of correlations, reducing all other physical properties to semi-illusory appearances of superpositional substates/dispositions. Objects and events are not physically determinate, only our mental records/experience of them. Whenever we speak of physical reality, we are really only ever speaking of correlations—correlations between correlations between correlations ad infinitum. Only the correlations are real. Only they can be said to objectively exist.

[39]

You have a concept of life that you correlate with a concept of death that you correlate with a concept of afterlife that you correlate with a concept of justice that you correlate with a concept of truth that you correlate with a concept of identity that you correlate with a concept of history that you correlate with a concept of memory that you correlate with a concept of mind that you correlate with a concept of brain that you correlate with a concept of body that you correlate with a concept of physicality that you correlate with a concept of physics that you correlate with a concept of math that you correlate with a concept of proof that you correlate with a concept of belief, and so on . . .

[40]

Observers are reliant on perception, and (human) perception is confined to a small section of the electromagnetic spectrum and bound by the speed of light, not to mention the restrictions dimensionality, mortality, and history/conditioning place upon us as observational systems. There has never been a pure/complete perception/observation, nor could there ever be.

[41]

Understood one way, the world is superpositional, not the mind. Understood another way, the mind is superpositional, not the world. Understood yet another way, world and mind are one and the same superposition, and still yet another way, there is no world or mind, only superpositional relationships within the omnipositional medium of the eidetic substratum.

[42]

Question: How real are determinate records/memory configurations?
Answer: They are as real as you need them to be.

[43]

Well-meaning skeptics might criticize/dismiss theories involving multiplicitous universes on the grounds that such theories fail to provide an adequate explanation of where other universes come from (i.e., the mechanics by which they branch/split/multiply), but these same critics should remember they themselves are lacking a definitive answer for how our own universe came into being, or from whence it arose. A thorough explanation/description of the process by which our universe materialized would necessarily provide answers to the process by which other universes materialize. But our subjective mortal humanoid perspective may prohibit us from ever gaining such complete insight, if such complete insight indeed exists.

[44]

Ten Ways a Multiverse Could Be

1. A universe could branch into multiple universal trajectories during a quantum measurement.
2. A universe could reflect itself as an infinity mirror, and its reflections could reflect themselves as infinity mirrors, and so on.

3. The universe does not branch into alternate universes, but your mind does.

4. Multiple universes could be holographically superimposed over one another like ghosts.

5. Multiple universes could be hyperspatially embedded within one another like the layers of an infinite onion.

6. Multiple universes could be physically scrunched up against one another like plant/skin cells.

7. Multiple universes could be bubbles of gravity distortion (i.e., time) spread out from one another across impassable gulfs of the universal substratum.

8. Anything could happen in a simulated reality (whether the simulation is computer-generated or a deific dream is another matter).

9. Multiple universes could simply be an interesting idea, but there is only one universe (the one in which you are currently reading this sentence).

10. The universe, as you conceive of it, does not exist. Our current conception of the universe (i.e., our conception based on the theory of relativity, the big bang theory and quantum mechanics) is barely a hundred years old. Who knows what the future will unveil?

[45]

There is no alpha universe, no first history, no prime you. Time is the falsified experience of determinate moments. All possible chronological sequences/ spatial configurations exist simultaneously in the omniposition, which means there is no initial set of superpositions. Time is an eidetic construct, the phenomenological byproduct of quantum decoherence.

[46]

Time is the projection of past, present, and future onto a roiling intermixture of transtemporal still life states.

Time is not continuous. The arrow of time is either omnidirectional, or there is no arrow.

[47]

Minds evolve to exploit the information within their particular field of awareness. Minds sufficiently compelled by environmental/social pressures will seek to widen their field of awareness.

[48]

You are quantumly entangled with all of the information that has ever come into contact with you (i.e., crossed your perceptual threshold). You are strongly correlated (in the quantum sense as well as the psychosocial sense) to your day-to-day environment, where you receive and relay the majority of your information. Your day-to-day environment is strongly correlated with the rest of the country, which is strongly correlated with the rest of the world, which is strongly correlated with the rest of the solar system, but beyond that the correlations grow weaker, as there is less informational interaction/influence. Information equals correlation, and it takes a long time for information to traverse the vast interstellar gulfs. All matter in the universe is presumably correlated to a slight degree through quantum entanglement, since all proto-matter was fused as one in the seed state before the Big Bang.

[49]

Different emotional frequencies yield different minds (i.e., self-similar systems that process and exploit information). Different minds yield different observers on different worldlines. The obvious takeaway here is that minds have the ability to influence (or possibly even select!) which world/universe they experience during any given temporal sequence, to a certain degree.

To change your mind is to change the world, because the world and the mind are synonymous.

[50]

If there are more than enough universes/histories to accommodate every possible combination of events (observations/measurements), and each is but an algorithm going through its predetermined/ preprogrammed calculations, then the only way we could have even a semblance of autonomy is if every observer were associated with continuously multiplying minds shifting fluidly between worldlines based on the observer's *willful* alterations of eidetic frequencies (i.e., conscious decisions/ choices), but what would be the use of such an extravagant process—merely to allay our egocentric insecurities? Is this a desperate attempt to hold onto our most prized possession—autonomy, our sense of free will, the privileged feeling that we alone among all matter in the cosmos are free to determine our own fate? Whether you have free will or not, your experience of reality still feels the same. However, belief in a lack of autonomy may cause an observer to interpret/perceive certain events differently than they would otherwise.

[51]

The eidetic substratum is omnivariant (as is time*, which is yet another eidetic and hence displays eidetic dynamical signatures such as omnivariance, entanglement, nonlinearity, multiplicity, relativity, fractality, and holographicality), but mental states have a curious habit of evolving into linear sequences of determinate information.

*The term *time* is employed here in a more robust sense than the speed of light, which is invariant, or the evolution of superpositional coordinate transformations, which are covariant.

[52]

Individual minds partake of the universal mind as well as form it. Sometimes the universal mind is referred to as the Eidos. More often it is referred to as the eidetic substratum.

[53]

If we all share the same mind, it would be sensible to work toward one of two goals:

A) We want what is best for ourselves, meaning what is best for everyone, so we work to create equality.

B) We want what is best for ourselves, meaning our particular mindset, so we work to eradicate every mindset that differs from ours.

Goal *A* evolves toward an adaptable mental resource base. Goal *B* evolves toward a non-adaptable mental resource base.

[54]

In the year 1899, Austrian neurologist Sigmund Freud (born: 1856 CE, died: 1939 CE) colonized the collective psyche of humanity and tried to commandeer all our dreams by defining the symbolisms and mechanisms of subconscious expression, publishing his seminal work, *The Interpretation of Dreams*. Freud explained that psychic energy (i.e., thoughts and moods, not clairvoyance and psychokinesis) is an actual form of energy, subject to the Law of Conservation of Energy, which states that energy can neither be created nor destroyed, it can only assume different manifestations. If negative psychic energy (which commonly results from mental and physical abuse) isn't *actively* released through positive channels (such as art, music, writing, prayer, community service, psychotherapy, etc.) it will *passively* express itself through negative channels of neurosis (such as depression, obsessive-compulsive disorder, and a wide variety of phobias). Neurosis is universal, according to Freud. Being a social animal takes its toll on us all. Freud believed the primary aim of psychoanalysis is to get you to consciously recognize and be honest about the embarrassing/shameful contents of your unconscious, which protects itself from scrutiny through misdirection and a self-inflicted form of amnesia. The way Freud talks about it, you'd think we have multiple minds.

[55]

Swiss psychoanalyst Carl Jung (born: 1875 CE, died: 1961 CE) was a short-term disciple of Sigmund Freud. Jung conjectured that our personalities are reducible to one of two mutually exclusive types of attitude combined with four faculties of cognition. The two polaric attitudes are "introversion" (the shy, quiet, loner type—those who focus their psychic energy inward) and "extroversion" (the outgoing, talkative, flirty type—those who focus their psychic energy outward), and the four cognitive faculties are: logic, intuition, emotion, and perception. Like his mentor Freud, Jung believed the human mind was a confluence of two distinct perceptual frames: the conscious and the unconscious. But Jung further divided the unconscious into the personal unconscious and the collective unconscious. The personal unconscious is the accumulation of repressed memories from our subjective history. The collective unconscious is the psychological imprint left by countless generations of evolution, a morphogenetic psychophysical residue. The very structure of our psyche has been shaped by the remote experiences of our many ancestral incarnations, sharing three billion years of common perceptions, like the daily appearance and disappearance of the sun and moon, the sensations of pain and pleasure (i.e., desire and fulfillment, i.e., tension and relief), and the anxiety of death.

[56]

In American hypnotherapist Carver Whittleton's (born: 1919 CE, died: 1991 CE) seminal work, *The Interpretation of Frank Holmestead's Interpretation of Sigmund Freud's Interpretation of Dreams*, the first chapter opens with this question: "What is a dream? An incoherent picture-puzzle? A prophecy from beyond? A secret message from you to yourself? The residue of recent stress? The residue of childhood trauma? The repercussion of something spicy you ate for dinner? An extradimensional brain fart? The orchestration of melatonin, oxytocin, acetylcholine, and dopamine? The haunting visitation of someone who recently died? A surreal distortion of unfulfilled desire? A surreal distortion of unresolved shame? Practice for gaining lucidity during the dreamlike experience associated with the moment of death? Evidence that conversations are going on in your mind without you knowing? Proof that your sense of self can be displaced from your body? An indication of the eidetic fabric of reality? The simple answer is yes." The final chapter of Whittleton's book ends with this passage: "Expressions of consciousness are born of subconscious expressions, which are born of personal unconscious expressions, which are born of collective unconscious expressions, which are born of evolutionary expressions, which are born of cosmic expressions. Therefore, consciousness is born of cosmic expressions. Consciousness is a cosmic expression."

[57]

The French philosopher Jean-Paul Sartre (born: 1905 CE, died: 1980 CE) claimed there was no ontologically privileged version of reality, no objective domain of understanding beyond human perception/comprehension/subjectivity. Reality is exactly what it appears to be (in the case of a human, specifically you), at least until someone convinces you the appearance is otherwise, and even then, reality will still *only* be what the new appearance appears to be. Reality is ultimately whatever you experience. We only see reality as we need in order to use it. It's not that reality (i.e., the world) isn't real, it's just that reality (i.e., the eidetic substratum) and the objects which comprise it are collections of limitless potential perceptions/experiences waiting to be perceived/experienced, and each one of us is limited to perceiving/experiencing only our own particular angles/insights/eidetics.

[58]

Belief in an objective reality (i.e., the reality of math and science with human subjectivity removed from the equation) is a modern-day form of mysticism.

[59]

The Fourfold Erasure (or the Tetrarasura): Any given conjecture/belief is true. The opposite of any given conjecture/belief is true. There is a deeper level of understanding in which any given conjecture/belief and its opposite are each true in their own way. There is a deeper level of understanding in which any given conjecture/belief and its opposite are each untrue in their own way.

[60]

Is phantom limb pain real? If you are experiencing phantom limb pain, then it is real to you. But this answer could also suffice for the experience of ghosts, angels, and pink elephants. Perhaps the question of phantom limb pain is best answered through an application of the Tetrarasura (the Fourfold Erasure): There is a sense in which phantom limb pain is real. There is a sense in which phantom limb pain is not real. There is a sense in which phantom limb pain is both real and unreal. There is a sense in which phantom limb pain is neither real nor unreal.*

*This does not mean only one of the four answers is correct (which would merely be an application of the standard tetralemma). The Tetrarasura is meant to demonstrate how each answer is correct yet limited in its own way, and only by considering them in totality does the fullest expression/interpretation of the truth become revealed.

[61]

If unicorns do not exist, then neither does the sense of this statement. If unicorns are not real, then how is it you are? You are as real as the unicorns you do not believe in.

[62]

There is no way to know if a system of logic has addressed every possible situation/context. At one point we were unaware of quantum mechanics. At one point we were unaware of relativity theory. At one point we were unaware of Newtonian physics. At one point we were unaware of Copernican heliocentrism. At one point we did not even have the concept of zero as we know it today. As opposed to capturing ultimate Truth, logical systems are better suited for proving expressions/equations inconsistent according to their rules for consistency. A logical system cannot assure immutable consistency over the long passage of time, and workability should never be confused for axiomatic/dogmatic certainty.

[63]

Whether or not I am supersymmetric strings and photons and atoms and molecules and electrochemical synapses in a brain in a vat in a holographic simulation in a hyperdimensional omniposition of the eidetic substratum, I am still sitting at the desk in my room, writing this sentence.

[64]

You are not the workings of your brain, nor are you an awareness field of recordable perceptions extending backward and forward in time unbound by space but not imagination. You are the concept of you, and the familiar feeling of that concept.

[65]

Reality is not only a concept—*reality is concept.* Reality at its most fundamental level is pure conceptuality.

[66]

Your mind is not something in your head. Rather, your head is something in your mind. But is it really *in* your mind? And is it really *your* mind?

[67]

In 1928, Edward Bernays, American pioneer of propaganda, published his seminal work,

Propaganda, in which he argues that public relations plays a crucial role in establishing/maintaining societal order. Here is an excerpt from the book: "The conscious and intelligent manipulation of the organized habits and opinions of the masses is an important element in democratic society. Those who manipulate this unseen mechanism of society constitute an invisible government which is the true ruling power of our country. We are governed, our minds molded, our tastes formed, and our ideas suggested, largely by men we have never heard of… it is they who pull the wires that control the public mind."

[68]

The Psychic War

There's a psychic war,
it's been going on
for about a hundred years.

You've probably never heard of it,
which means they're winning.

It's being waged
through weapons of mass distraction
and weapons of mass division
and weapons of mass discouragement
and weapons of mass dismissal,
and it's about to get worse,
much worse.

Tinfoil hats aren't enough anymore.
We must don tinfoil suits of armor.

[69]
Mediatized

I want you to listen to what I'm saying.
Really listen.
How can I take your mind?

I repeat, how can I take your mind?

You probably don't realize it, but
I have just taken your mind.
It's mine now.

I want you to imagine a green gorilla.
Seriously, imagine a green gorilla.

Even if you resist my command,
you'll only be struggling not to see
a green gorilla.

Do you understand?
This is how they get you, buy you, sell you.

You are the price of your attention.

Green gorillas don't exist,

yet now they do, to me and you,

whether true or not.

Here, take your mind back.

Go give it to some other stranger.

[70]

Remote Viewing Protocol Checklist

1. Am I reading subtle cues from the tester's body language?
2. Am I finding the answer in the crosshairs of extremely developed intuition and empathy (but then I should also ask what intuition and empathy really consist of)?
3. Am I perceiving the answer from the tester's own mind's eye?
4. Am I reading the tester's mind?

5. Am I astrally relocating my locus of consciousness to a different angle from which I can see the answer?

6. Am I relocating my own consciousness into an altogether different universe (a different superposition of the universal wavelength) where the answer is the one which I have chosen?

7. Am I manifesting the reality which conforms to my answer by sheer force of will?

8. Am I sensitive to near-imperceptible signals both molecular and atomic (and possibly even subatomic) which allow me to focus my answer in one direction as opposed to another?

9. Am I uncannily good at making lucky guesses?

10. Am I predicting what the answer will be revealed as in the future?

11. Am I honing in on the coordinates of the transtemporal field of universal consciousness that contain my answer?

12. Am I sensing psychic impressions in the present, or am I warping time?

13. Am I experiencing the correct answer through myself at a later time?

14. Am I asleep and attempting to find the answer while lucid dreaming?

15. Am I piggybacking on the psychic ability of my moderator or evaluator, or drawing upon their limited psychic reserves to augment my own?

16. Is my location on the planet currently facing away from the center of the Milky Way Galaxy?

17. Am I attempting to divine the answer at the auspicious hour, on the auspicious day?

18. Am I tuning into the frequency of a specific star or pulsar or quasar or position of stars or some other mysterious cosmic entity/force/phenomenon?

19. Is the CIA somehow transmitting the answer into my brain, testing out their latest sonic weaponry, or possibly the KGB?

20. Am I receiving the answer from God?

21. Am I receiving the answer from the devil?

[71]

From French philosopher Michel Foucault's (born: 1926 CE, died: 1984 CE) *Discipline & Punish: The Birth of the Prison*: "He who is subjected to a field of visibility, and who knows it, assumes responsibility for the constraints of power; he makes them play spontaneously upon himself; he inscribes in himself the power relation in which he simultaneously plays both roles; he becomes the principle of his own subjection." In other words, if you believe an authority figure is watching you, you will police yourself.

[72]

Two passages from French Marxist philosopher Guy Debord's (born: 1931 CE, died: 1994 CE) *The Society of the Spectacle*:

Thesis 1:

In societies where modern conditions of production prevail, all of life presents itself as an immense accumulation of *spectacles*. Everything that was directly lived has moved away into representation.

Thesis 218:

The spectator's consciousness, imprisoned in a flattened universe, bound by the *screen* of the spectacle behind which his life has been deported, knows only the *fictional* speakers who unilaterally surround him with their commodities and the politics of their commodities. The spectacle, in its entirety, is his "mirror image."

[73]

Your mind is not hiding somewhere
between your ears.

Your mind isn't even yours.
We're all sharing it.

But like most things that can be shared,
some want it all for themselves.

[74]

On average, there are sixteen minutes of commercials
for every hour of programming. The average child
spends an average of six hours per day watching
television, exposing them to ninety-six minutes of
commercials every day. This means the average child
has spent well over five thousand hours downloading
consumerist propaganda into his or her receptive
brain by the time they are ten years of age—well over

five thousand hours of deceptive demoralizing advertising tactics drilled into their defenseless minds during the formative years, and this is only the commercials, to say nothing of the dubious content of the programs they are watching *between* the commercials.

[75]

Israeli psychologist Daniel Kahneman (born: 1934 CE, died: probably by the time you read this): "The confidence people have in their beliefs is not a measure of the quality of evidence but of the coherence of the story that the mind has managed to construct."

Ask yourself: Why do I believe the things I believe? The not-so-right answer: I believe the things I believe because the things I believe are correct. The righter answer: I believe the things I have been conditioned to believe because the things I have been conditioned to believe have not totally failed me yet. The rightest answer: Everything I believe is false, but I am generally in denial, and anyway, the show must go on.

[76]

sanity (noun): the ability to think and behave in a normal and rational manner; sound mental health (according to who? the Nazis? the Spanish inquisitors? the Sicilian Mafia? the Scientologists? the Donald Trump supporters? the Christian fundamentalists? the atheists? the psychological community? your local community? the commercials on television?).

[77]

Sanity is overtly eidetic, and so is insanity. There is no such objectively factual state as "sanity," or even "collective normativity." One can directly know/perceive whether one is happy or sad or angry. One cannot directly know/perceive whether one is sane or insane. The ever-shifting concepts of sanity and insanity are simply useful eidetics for managing/harmonizing societies (i.e., large groups of minds) through the regulation of the collective experience of reality. Everyone in every era is un-sane, and the most sane behavior one can partake in is to study our various modes of un-sanity. If the rules and restrictions (the guidelines?) of sanity are based on that which makes a society flourish over the long term, then it is clear that every modern-day society is inflicted with multiple strains of insanity.

In the words of German psychologist Erich Fromm (born: 1900 CE, died: 1980 CE): "It is naively assumed that the fact that the majority of people share certain ideas or feelings proves the validity of these ideas and feelings. Nothing is further from the truth . . . Just as there is a *folie à deux*, there is a *folie à millions*. The fact that millions of people share the same vices does not make these vices virtues, the fact that they share so many errors does not make the errors to be truths, and the fact that millions of people share the same form of mental pathology does not make these people sane." —*The Sane Society*, Routledge, 1955, pp.14–15.

[78]

Scottish philosopher David Hume believes we only have access to impressions, which affect us according to their level of force and vivacity, which are determined by the valuation system of the society one is predominantly conditioned/influenced by. An impression is a way of representing something, of simulating it.

[79]

In 2003, Swedish philosopher Nick Bostrom proposed *The Simulation Argument*, claiming that one of these three unlikely propositions is almost certainly true:

1. The fraction of human-level civilizations that reach a posthuman stage (that is, one capable of running high-fidelity ancestor simulations) is very close to zero.

2. The fraction of posthuman civilizations that are interested in running simulations of their evolutionary history, or variations thereof, is very close to zero.

3. The fraction of all people with our kind of experiences that are living in a simulation is very close to one.

If the third proposition turns out to be true, then we are almost certainly living in a simulation. But of course we are living in a simulation, on at least two distinct levels: sensorial (by which we are simulated) and conceptual (by which we are simulators). What does computational add to the equation?* And who's to say the reality behind the simulation is not itself a simulation, and so on ad infinitum. It is enough to realize that reality is eidetic. Everything is ideation/hallucination/simulation.

*American economist Robin Hanson has some strangely pragmatic advice for anyone who believes they are living in a (computerized) simulation: characters in a high-fidelity simulation should strive to be entertaining and praiseworthy in order to avoid being switched off, cancelled, or relegated to the role of a semiconscious (or even nonconscious) low-fidelity NPC (non-player character).

[80]
Everything in the universe is a quantum computer, including the universe itself.

[81]

The intentional aspect of mind could very well stem from the morphogenetic residue of primordial attractions and repulsions instilled during our evolution from star to sentient ape, built into our cerebral hardware, which would explain the difficulty duplicating its presence through humanmade software, as a computer can only *simulate* this millennia-long process of gradual intentionality at best . . . unless what we consider intentionality isn't intentional at all. Intentionality is eidetic (like everything else, including this sentence). The mechanisms/processes that lead to the experience of volition are so unfathomably complex that we are most likely perceiving/conceptualizing their workings as something altogether different. Intentionality could simply be the *feeling* that results from a quantum supercomputer simulating quadrillions of scenarios (or perhaps infinite, depending on whether one prefers in this context to think of quantum supercomputers in terms of brains or universes) per second while calculating probabilities. If infinite scenarios are continuously playing out, there is a 100% probability that everything you will ever possibly think, say, and do is precisely described by one or more simulations, depending on whether infinity is infinitely varied or repeats itself ad nauseum.

[82]

Medieval theologians debated over how many angels could dance on the head of pin, which seemed ludicrous to astronomers and physicists of the Renaissance. In the 21st century, logicians claim with confidence that ten million hydrogen atoms can fit snugly on the head of a pin.

[83]

Perhaps this passage from philosopher Thomas Aquinas' *Summa Theologica* will shed some light on the subject of angels and hyperdimensional mechanics (except all instances of the word *angel* have been replaced with the word *mind*):

"It is befitting [a mind] to be in a place; yet [a mind] and a body are said to be in a place in quite a different sense. A body is said to be in a place in such a way that it is applied to such place according to the contact of dimensive quantity; but there is no such quantity in the [mind], for [minds are] virtual. Consequently [a mind] is said to be in a corporeal place by application of the [mental] power in any manner whatever to any place.

Accordingly there is no need for saying that [a mind] can be deemed commensurate with a place, or that it occupies a space in the continuous; for this is proper to a located body which is endowed with dimensive quantity. In similar fashion it is not necessary on this account for the [mind] to be contained by a place; because an incorporeal substance virtually contains the thing with which it comes into contact, and is not contained by it: for the [mind] is in the body as containing it, not as contained by it. In the same way [a mind] is said to be in a place which is corporeal, not as the thing contained, but as somehow containing it."

[84]

The Eidetics of Language

Every proposition/description/explanation involves five frameworks/lenses/filters of meaning:

1. Your intended meaning.

2. Your unintended meaning(s).

3. The grammatological meaning(s) inherent in your statement.

4. The echoes of intertextual references and lingo-genetic substructures.

5. The audience's interpretation of your meaning, which takes into account any and all subjectively relevant contexts (cultural, geographical, historical, environmental, political, social, psychological, moral, sexual, and so on).

[85]

Austrian-British philosopher Ludwig Wittgenstein (born: 1889 CE, died: 1951 CE) wrote "to imagine a language means to imagine a form of life." Accordingly he believed "all philosophy is a critique of language" and "the sole remaining task for philosophy is the analysis of language."

[86]

The Telephone Game

We exist in the liminal
between language and perception.

Mind is all around you,

thinking you into being.

Language is all around you,

speaking you into this world.

[87]

Languages are hive-minded parasites with the power to appear as infinite cosmoses. Language is not an extension of you. You are an extension of language.

[88]

The difference between an illusion and an eidetic is that an eidetic can arrest you.

[89]

Beliefs relate to eidetics the way letters relate to words.

[90]

Question: Is everything eidetic?

Answer: Hope and doubt motivate all eidetics, but are themselves not eidetic, because hope and doubt are based on the cognizant uncertainty of belief.

[91]

The "deepest mysteries of reality" are eidetic. Everything in reality is deeply mysterious, but only to us. The fundamental nature of an apple is unknowable, yet its sweetness is immediately available, and its nourishment. The "fundamental nature" of anything is an eidetic maze.

[92]

<u>Prehistory</u>: Nature presents various autocentric models of the cosmos.

<u>Earliest recorded history BCE</u>: Our ancient forebears present various theocentric models of the cosmos.

<u>Circa 600 BCE</u>: Thales presents the water model of

the cosmos (i.e., everything is made of water).

<u>Circa 575 BCE</u>: Anaximander presents the apeiron model of the cosmos (i.e., everything is made of an everlasting substance that cannot be directly experienced/perceived).

<u>Circa 550 BCE</u>: Anaximenes presents the air model of the cosmos (i.e., everything is made of air).

<u>Circa 530 BCE</u>: Pythagoras presents the numeric/mathematical model of the cosmos (coining the term *kosmos* to describe the beautiful order he observes in the starry heavens).

<u>Circa 500 BCE</u>: Heraclitus presents the fire model of the cosmos (i.e., everything is made of fire).

<u>Circa 450 BCE</u>: Empedocles presents the fourfold elemental model of the cosmos (i.e., everything is made of four basic elements: fire, air, earth, and water).

<u>Circa 400 BCE</u>: Democritus presents the atomistic model of the cosmos.

<u>Circa 130 CE</u>: Ptolemy presents the geocentric model

of the cosmos.

<u>1543 CE</u>: Nicolaus Copernicus presents the heliocentric model of the cosmos.

<u>1687 CE</u>: Isaac Newton presents the gravitational model of the cosmos.

<u>1915 CE</u>: Albert Einstein presents the relativistic model of the cosmos.

<u>1927 CE</u>: Georges Lemaitre presents the Big Bang model of the cosmos.

<u>1956 CE</u>: Hugh Everett III presents the multiversal model of the cosmos.

<u>1978 CE</u>: Gerard 't Hooft, Leonard Susskind, and Charles Thorn present the holographic model of the cosmos.

<u>1984 CE</u>: Alexei Starobinski and Yakov Borisovich Zeldovich present the three-torus model (a.k.a. the donut-shaped model) of the cosmos.

<u>1995 CE</u>: Edward Witten presents the M-theory model of the cosmos (i.e., everything is made of supersymmetric strings vibrating in eleven

dimensions).

<u>2003 CE</u>: Nick Bostrom presents the simulation model of the cosmos.

<u>2012 CE</u>: Thoth de Miurgé presents the eidocentric model of the cosmos (i.e., reality manifests/behaves according to the intellect and sensibilities of its practitioners).

<u>2020 CE</u>: Sophia Mercury presents the superorganism model of the cosmos (i.e., the universe is a living organism and we are its organs of thought).

Do you really believe our journey of discovery has reached its conclusion?

[93]

An organism is any self-enclosed system with an organized structure that can react to stimuli, reproduce, grow, adapt, and maintain homeostasis, functioning as an individual entity. According to this standard definition of an organism, the Earth could be considered an organism, as could the universe. The most abundant elements that make up the human body—hydrogen, oxygen, nitrogen, and carbon—are also among the most common elements that make up the universe, which should hardly come as a surprise. We are a superorganism of the multitudinous cells in our body, and the universe is a strange reflection of us, albeit on a much grander scale. The universe was born (during the Big Bang/Entropic Ejaculation). The universe grows, reproducing "baby universes" (a term coined by physicist Stephen Hawking) through the formation of black holes. The universe adapts; we are living proof of this. The universe ages, and eventually dies. Individual neurons may enact their individual synaptic computations, but our mind experiences the outcome as a unified expression, and the universe is a strange reflection of us, or more accurately, we are a strange reflection of the universe.

[94]

The multiverse is a compact aggregate of universal superorganisms devouring and birthing one another. Universal superorganisms have the capacity to communicate with other universal superorganisms, but they rarely do so. Imagine our universe resembles an amoeba, and sentient beings form/express its mind (in both an individualistic manner and a collective manner through quantum entanglement on a macrocosmic scale) while its material form (its body) develops and matures according to the laws of nature for its species, certain aspects of which may vary from universe to universe. Every universe is a reincarnation. Our universe is past its prime, having grown very cold.

[95]

What we normally think of as objects—tables, trees, electrons, stars, brains—are in fact properties of the universal superorganism.

[96]

The universal superorganism expresses itself through stars and planets and our brains, its omnipresent voice borne on rippling gravity. A vast transdimensional computer, the universal superorganism generates seemingly infinite possible courses of action, all of the realities in which we or anything else will ever exist, each of which is quasi-real, never deciding on a single scenario, never reaching a conclusion. The universal superorganism doesn't differentiate between dreaming and thinking and imagining, the distinctions of which are purely eidetic.

[97]

Aurelius Augustinus of Hippo, a.k.a. Saint Augustine (born: 354 CE, died: 430 CE), was a Medieval religious philosopher who claimed that science is a disease of curiosity that inspires men to search out the hidden powers of nature for their own perversion. He believed God created time and omnisciently knew how everything in the cosmos was going to unfold. Thus, God is abstracted from time while being time itself. Augustine contemplated temporal subjects pertaining to theology, such as how reality existed before God invented time, or why God conceived of Creation after an eternity of nothingness? He wondered how anyone could possess free will if everything we do is preordained according to God's plan, and how could God hold us responsible for what we do, when we are ultimately predestined to do it? How can a future that does not yet exist be predictable, or prophesied with any degree of precognition? To answer these questions, Augustine divided time into two categories: God's time and our time. Our time consists of the everyday experience of past, present, and future. This sequential ordering of events only exists in our minds. Only the present is real. The past is a current memory, and the future is just a present expectation. In his own words: "But what now is manifest and clear is, that neither are there future nor past things. Nor is it right to say, 'There are three times: past, present and future.' But it might be right to say, 'There are three times: a present of things past, a present of things present, and a present of things future.' For these three times do somehow exist in the soul." Seconds, minutes, hours, days, months, years, centuries—these are simply ways of applying order to our present experience. Our time is comprised from incremental changes/moments with beginnings and ends. But God's time (eternity/infinity) is the perception of all time simultaneously. God's time is an unchanging and boundless totality, never starting, never ending, incapable of being separated into this or that timeframe, viewing the whole picture of everything that will ever be. Augustine's segregated conception of time provided him with satisfactory answers to his metaphysical questions: What was God doing before He created the world? In God's time, there is no before the creation of the world. As God sees it, the world has always been part of His grand scheme. Regarding the question of how someone (like a prophet) could know the future before it happens, God knows the entire book of reality, and sometimes He reveals portions of the story which are yet to come, but only to those who will help achieve the objective(s) of His storyline. This means God does not control the outcomes of our stories. He merely knows them. Does this imply God did not write the book of reality, or that He wrote it in a sort of trance? And if God reveals portions of the story which are yet to come, is this tantamount to breaking the fourth wall? Have these metafictional cameos always been part of the story, or can God revise what He has written? Of all the eidetics, anthropomorphic God is the most tantalizing.

[98]

Saint Augustine believed the present moment is a duration of time so short it cannot be subdivided any further.

[99]

Saint Thomas Aquinas (born: 1225 CE, died: 1274 CE) was an Italian Dominican friar who did much to reconcile the Church's distrust of science, but obviously not enough. His parents wanted him to pursue a noble Italian career as a young man. When he disclosed his intention to become a wandering mendicant, his parents imprisoned him in their fortress for two years, trying to persuade him to change his mind. Their efforts failed. Eventually his monk buddies came to the rescue by smuggling him out of the house in a large basket. Brother Aquinas alleviated some of the tension between faith and reason (i.e., religion and the philosophical sciences), establishing both as having their respective places in the realm of knowledge. Philosophy and science should be employed to study the tangible world of the senses. Faith and religion exist to understand the unseen world of the spirit.

Saint Thomas presented five contentions for the existence of God, believing these arguments amounted to indisputable evidence. The first contention states that if you follow every event to its preceding event, you will eventually reach a phenomenon that initiated all other events without itself being initiated—the Uncaused Cause. The second contention states that anything which moves was moved by something prior. If you trace back all of the forces instigating movement, you will eventually arrive at the initial source of all action—the Unmoved Mover. The third contention states that things must come from other things. If you follow the chain of manifestation all the way back to its source, you will eventually arrive at an initial thing that materialized out of nowhere/nothing. Since nothingness could not have created anything of its own accord, something must have caused the initial thing to occur. The fourth contention states that everything in nature (except humanity) behaves according to certain pre-established laws. Everything in nature seems to unwittingly know its role. Saint Thomas believed this was proof that something/someone must be conducting/overseeing the grand design of the cosmos. The fifth contention states that because we have knowledge regarding abstract concepts such as perfection and eternity, but can find none of their examples in reality, we must be apprehending essences from the actual manifestations/wellsprings of these concepts.

[100]

Zeno of Elea (circa 450 BCE) worked on understanding duration and the nature of the present moment. Being a student of Parmenides, he considered the senses to be deceitful, believing only pure reason can ascertain truth. Zeno's Paradox simplified: suppose we set up a hypothetical situation where someone must travel from point A to point B

by successive increments of 50%. How long would it take for the person to arrive at their destination? According to the logic of the hypothetical, the person will never arrive. Mathematical division can subdivide infinitely between any two points. Zeno thought of time as a continuous loop, meaning there will be infinite reflections of this lifetime in the future, just as there have been infinite reflections of this lifetime in the past.

[101]

The ABCs of Collective Identity

If a letter-minded vessel posits A, it is only a matter of time and circumstance before another letter-minded vessel counters with $-A$ and/or B. And once B has been posited, another letter-minded vessel will eventually come along and posit $-B$ and/or C. The identity of the letter-minded vessel is inconsequential. The posits in this example take on a life of their own, conducting their own dialectic independent of any particular vessels. The next iteration could be posited by John Doe today, or John Smith a hundred years from now; the conversation/argument continues so long as another relevant letter-minded posit is posited. History and context are the true voice of the posit, not the letter-minded vessel, who is only a messenger/interpreter.

[102]

Thoughts exist in the world before anyone thinks/hears/speaks them. There is nothing mystical about this statement.

[103]

The Greek philosopher Empedocles (circa 450 BCE) introduced the theory (based upon faulty reasoning, according to today's standards) that all matter is made of four basic elements: fire, air, earth, and water. Furthermore, he determined (using faulty reasoning, according to today's standards) there are two fundamental forces that govern the elements: love and strife, i.e., attraction and repulsion (not unlike magnetism and gravity). Empedocles believed all matter is imbued with consciousness, and in a way he was right, but not in the way he meant. Quite ahead of his time, Empedocles determined (using faulty reasoning, according to today's standards) that light travels at a phenomenal speed but cannot manifest instantaneously (i.e., travel infinitely fast), as was commonly believed. He also determined (using faulty reasoning, according to today's standards) that organisms evolved into their current forms through a process of spontaneous mutation and adaptation. Perhaps in two thousand years our future selves will determine that every theory we held true in the 21st century was based on faulty reasoning.

[104]

Three Types of Time Travel*

1. Memory

1½. The Eidetic Afterlife Hypothesis (i.e., the hyper-dilation of dream time that occurs during the dying brain process, due to a restriction of oxygen, the release of powerful neurochemicals associated with dreams and hallucinations, a massive surge of synaptic excitation resulting in overload, and the shutdown of various centers of the brain responsible for our sense of the passage of time)

2. Experiential comparisons between different relativistic timeframes (in the physiological sense as well as the Einsteinian sense, which allows for time travel into the future**)

2½. Instantaneous informational relay (i.e., faster-than-light travel; i.e., teleportation; i.e., quantum entanglement; i.e., spooky action at a distance)

3. Exploiting porous membranes within one's universal superorganism (i.e., harnessing black holes or manufacturing wormholes) to "tunnel" from the current region of the space-time continuum to an earlier or later region **OR** "jumping" from one universal superorganism's timeline to a neighboring universal superorganism's timeline, shifting/traveling to a younger or older version/reflection/history of one's universal superorganism

3½. Fully immersive computer-generated simulations of past or future events

*Aside from our one-directional (causally forward) experience of the movement of objects/events (i.e., our common perception/conception of time and entropy), also known as "clock time" (i.e., external-world chronometrical increments denoting the sequential permutation of objects and their interrelationships).

** Time dilates/stretches for an object approaching

the speed of light relative to the reference (i.e., the inertial frame) of a stationary object. This explains why the "Twin Paradox" thought experiment is no paradox at all. The Twin Paradox supposes that one of a set of identical twins travels at near-light speed to a distant star, only to discover upon his return to Earth that his twin has aged more rapidly than himself, i.e., his identical twin is objectively older than him now. The paradox merely stems from a failure to understand certain consequences of special relativity theory that apply to objects traveling at near-light speeds. Regardless, the thought experiment demonstrates that time travel is indeed possible, but only in the forward sense of traveling to one's future.

[105]

Causality is eidetic. David Hume (born: 1711 CE, died: 1776 CE) was a very skeptical Scottish philosopher who claimed that everything is just a matter of perception and opinion. There is no such thing as matter-of-fact knowledge, according to Hume, only immediate and limited sensory data. All knowledge is derived from sensory experiences, but the senses are imperfect and bias, which prevents them from providing us with objective information. Everything we experience has been filtered/translated through our human-oriented perceptions. We cannot escape our subjectivity. All we will ever know of reality is our own reflection. Hume advanced the notion that the mind is not a real thing-in-the-world, and what is normally referred to as the mind is actually just a collection of experiences made coherent through memory. While studying the sequential nature of cause and effect, he deduced that causality is merely a psychological conditioning (of expectation and order) that arises from the reinforcement of recognized patterns.

The world is not a real thing-in-the-world.

[106]

Everything we hold true is merely the shadow play of a more fundamental, more real, eternal world of perfect essences/ideas/forms, according to Plato of Athens (circa 400 BCE). He believed the perfect beauty in nature was manifested through polyhedral shapes (i.e., geometry). Plato saw fire as a quivering tetrahedron, the Earth as a cube, air as formed of octahedrons, water as composed of icosahedrons, and the entire cosmos as contained in a dodecahedron. Plato understood that for any motion or change to occur, there must be empty space. But space is not empty in his view—space is the underlying substructure out of which all material substances are composed, a chaotic matrix of potentials from which order emerges in the form of stabilized matter, an invisible soup where things blink in and out of existence. Thus, even though all things appear separate and distinct, everything is united. Every form is a formation of space within space. Seemingly individual objects/entities are just manifestations of a single ubiquitous field, which would later be reconceived as the eidetic substratum.

[107]

Only the medium of interaction is objectively real-in-itself, i.e., only the eidetic substratum is un-eidetic, not that which the eidetic substratum concerns/constructs. Reality is a maelstrom of eidetics subservient to our individual and collective will. We are more than human. We are infinite potential. We are eidos. Humanity/humanness is merely another eidetic.

First-person POV is actually third-person POV, and vice versa.

[108]

Drex Postularis (born: 138 CE, died: 204 CE) was a Roman clockmaker (of clepsydras, or water clocks) who asserted that if space exists, then only movement and the decay/erosion arising from friction exist, therefore time is a fiction. But if time exists, then only the ubiquitous process of transformation exists, therefore space is a fiction.

[109]

Henry of Ghent (born: 1217 CE, died: 1293 CE) was a religious thinker who conjectured that time exists as a continuum independently of human thought, and we can never perceive it in its true present moment; our finite minds can only recognize time as earlier or later segments.

[110]

Duns Scotus (born: 1266 CE, died: 1308 CE) was a Scottish Franciscan friar and philosopher who argued that time must flow in a linear manner (as opposed to circular) which starts with an initial cause and ends with an ultimate fulfillment. He reasoned that no effect can cause itself, therefore, any effect must have been produced by some sort of cause, leading down a long causal chain straight to the source of all causes, i.e., the beginning of time. Even those who argue that time is a random mistake or imbalance of extradimensional harmony must realize an accident or imbalance can only occur in a system that is already ordered. Scotus divided time into two senses: physical and psychological. Physical time is the objective transformation of reality. Psychological time is our subjective experience of physical time.

[111]

Henri Bergson (born: 1859 CE, died: 1941 CE) was a French philosopher who said the essence of life is time, and by conditioning the mind, any person could fundamentally alter their perception of time, and therefore reality. It is the (human) mind's normal habit to divide moments into frozen segments, like movie stills on a roll of motion-picture film. But of course reality is not segmented; time is a continuous fluidity. In *Matter and Memory*, Bergson writes, "To perceive means to immobilize . . . we seize, in the act of perception, something which outruns perception itself." The (human) mind works backwards, taking the completed whole and breaking it down into simpler parts in order to build it back up in a way we can comprehend. The (human) mind continuously summons the past through disconnected petrified memories in an effort to navigate/manipulate future events, while nature is always perfectly in the present. Our nearsighted consciousness stands before the entire mosaic of reality but can only make out a small section of the brighter threads. Henri wondered what the experience of time would be like to a mind which had no concept of temporality (i.e., chronometrical measurement), in other words, to perceive time without stopping it. He contended there were two understandings of time: true time and pragmatic time. True time is the experience of the interconnectedness of duration; it's how we actually perceive time, with the past, present, and future all melding into our awareness. Our consciousness is an amalgam of ongoing sensations intermingled with recollections of events in the past and anticipations of events in the future. We have been conditioned to believe that every action in the present has an expected (i.e., directly connected) outcome in the future. Time is the combining of new data with old data, it's purely mental, according to Bergson. He said human consciousness is a forever changing experience, with no two moments ever experienced as the same, for the consciousness of one moment will always contain at least a trace of the consciousness preceding that moment due to the residue of memory. Pragmatic time consists of all the manmade quantifications we graph onto the world/universe in order to make it more comprehensible (i.e., manipulatable). Pragmatic time is the measure of space and movement, mathematical time. Bergson argued that mathematics does not accurately depict reality or time. Calculus is a fiction of logic; an object doesn't transition from point to point in temporal increments—it bleeds through all the points in its path, never being exactly here or there, but always in the whereabouts of the flow. Points in time don't really exist; there is only the drive of matter to constantly change. He claimed that time and space are separate phenomena with different attributes, even though they have identical applications. Space relates to the momentary juxtaposition of objects. Time is the process by which space unfolds into novel manifestations; time is the expression of reality's creativity. As we flow through the ever-changing timestream, the only experience that can be said to endure is the awareness/feeling that we are ourselves. Bergson believed that consciousness was mostly memory, which enables us to continue through one state to the next with cognitive coherency. He stated there were two types of memory processes. The most rudimentary form of memory is motor memory, such as the autonomic regulation of bodily functions. This is purely mechanical memory, the memory of biological necessity. The second type of memory can more appropriately be called remembrance, defined here as the recollection of events/experiences that occurred in time and space. Bergson also claimed there are two types of understanding. The first is awareness through intellect: what the mind correlates with an object, based on prior definitions and experiences. Intellect can only understand external attributes/qualities. The second type of understanding is intuition, which Bergson defines as "a simple, indivisible experience of sympathy through which one is moved into the inner being of an object to grasp what is unique and ineffable within it," adding that intuition is an evolved form of instinct which can dislocate itself from its immediate sensory perceptions. What separates mankind from the animals, according to Bergson, is that animals can only react to the stimuli of their surroundings, whereas humans have developed the ability to transcend ourselves and our environment. We can stand outside ourselves and reflect on ourselves as an object or event. Bergson defined God simply as the force of all life, always striving to express itself through ever more articulate forms.

[112]

How could time have a beginning and an end while also being infinite? For all given purposes time began with the Big Bang. If the universe ever stops expanding and begins to contract, it will eventually shrink to a state identical to that of its birth, reaching a point of infinite density, which some theorists have called the Big Crunch, upon which time (and space) will cease to be measurable for all given purposes, meaning time will end. But those who believe in the possibility of the Big Crunch also believe in the possibility of the Big Bounce, that the universe will explode forth again, setting time in motion anew. In this manner, time could be understood to have a beginning and an end while also continuing unto infinity.

Thus the issue dissolves under the Fourfold Erasure: It can be reasonably said that time has a beginning and an end. It can be reasonably said that time has no beginning and no end. It can be reasonably said that time does and does not have a beginning and an end. Therefore, our understanding of time must be amended.

[113]

Hermann Minkowski (born: 1864 CE, died: 1909 CE) was a German-Polish-Lithuanian-Russian mathematician who demonstrated that time and space variables should be calculated using the same coordinate system. He turned the typical notion of geometric reality from a 3-dimensional understanding of area to our modern concept of a 4-dimensional space-time continuum. This means there are three dimensions of volumetric space (height, width, and depth), plus one more dimension to indicate relativistic transformations of events within the space. Empty space is 3-D, anything interacting in space is 4-D. Time is the 4th dimension. When plotting trajectories on a chart, every point represents an event which happens in time and space. To flow through time is to change locations in space, and moving through space takes time.

[114]

German mathematician Theodore Kaluza (born: 1885 CE, died: 1954 CE) and Swedish physicist Oskar Klein (born: 1894 CE, died: 1977 CE) theorized the possibility of a minutely unobservable extra dimension curled up within every particle of our observable four-dimensional phenomena. They formulated equations based on five interactive dimensions of reality, discovering that their calculations solved a conundrum which had beset physicists for years, namely the difficulty in relating small-scale subatomic behavior with large-scale relativistic behavior. Kaluza and Klein worked out a mathematical theory that could explain both gravity and electromagnetism through the introduction of an undetectable extra spatial dimension. This fifth dimension is wound into a compact sphere (like rolling a length of string into a ball) so infinitesimal that it fails to have a noticeable effect on extremely microscopic expressions of reality, yet its all-pervasive underlying presence exhibits a synergistic influence over the behavior of matter at the macroscopic scale. The involuted fifth dimension, if it exists, would have to be significantly smaller than the nucleus of an atom.

[115]

Dimensionality evolves alongside our understanding. The concept of a sixth dimension arises from the multiversal interpretation of quantum mechanics. The sixth dimension encapsulates the set of parallel universes/histories resulting solely from our particular universe's initial conditions (i.e., the Big Bang). The seventh dimension concerns all possible universes. Some theorists have seen fit to divide the fourth dimension (the dimension of time) into two distinct dimensions, one that addresses forward temporal movement, and one that addresses backward temporal movement, because particles behave differently (i.e., exhibit different properties) under different temporal modes. In mathematics, octonions have eight dimensions and form an 8-dimensional vector space with applications in string theory, special relativity, and quantum computing. Superstring theory claims the fabric of space-time is 10-dimensional, while M-theory concludes it to be 11-

dimensional, and bosonic string theory argues for twenty-six dimensions! Last year the idea of 24-dimensionality was in vogue. This year it's 33⅓.

and thus

the foundation

of reality

is built

on eidetics

[116]

Brain states may be triggered by other brain states (such as making a decision) as well as stimuli from the outer world. A brain state will never indicate/ describe a specific expression of thought/mind, for such expressions are dynamic, epiphenomenal (but in a more robust sense of the word, i.e., causally efficacious) and transdimensional, like everything else that arises from the eidetic substratum. Reality is certainly real, but real is only quasi-real, or real enough to act upon.

[117]

The outer world is an eidetic concept.

Brain states are an eidetic concept.

Intentionality is an eidetic concept.

The words themselves create eidetic mazes.

[118]

A) The experience of the green afterimage of the red color field is eidetic.

B) The green afterimage of the red color field is eidetic.

C) The redness of the red color field is eidetic.

[119]

A function is defined by its role in the operation of a system. The operational process of any given function is interdependent upon the operational processes of other functions. Functions are multiply realizable;

i.e., there are many (perhaps infinite) ways to fulfill the role/operation of any given function. A brain need not be made of neurons to produce a mind. The brain is a device for recognizing symbols*, and the mind is a program for manipulating concepts. There is no manipulation of concepts without the recognition of symbols. Symbols come from the world. Symbols make up the world. Symbols have intentional content. Symbols speak the mind into being.

*A symbol in this context could mean: a physical tree, the mental image of a tree, the picture (drawing, painting, photo) of a tree, the written word *tree*, or an utterance of the word, "tree."

[120]
American philosopher John R. Searle's (born: 1932 CE, died: probably by the time you read this) argument on the implausibility of artificial intelligence: "Suppose that I'm locked in a room and

given a large batch of Chinese writing. Suppose furthermore (as is indeed the case) that I know no Chinese, either written or spoken, and that I'm not even confident that I could recognize Chinese writing as Chinese writing distinct from, say, Japanese writing or meaningless squiggles. To me, Chinese writing is just so many meaningless squiggles. Now suppose further that after this first batch of Chinese writing I am given a second batch of Chinese script together with a set of rules for correlating the second batch with the first batch. The rules are in English, and I understand these rules as well as any other native speaker of English. They enable me to correlate one set of formal symbols with another set of formal symbols, and all that 'formal' means here is that I can identify the symbols entirely by their shapes. Now suppose also that I am given a third batch of Chinese symbols together with some instructions, again in English, that enable me to correlate elements of this third batch with the first two batches, and these rules instruct me how to give back certain Chinese symbols with certain sorts of shapes in response to certain sorts of shapes given me in the third batch. Unknown to me, the people who are giving me all of these symbols call the first batch a 'script,' they call the second batch a 'story,' and they call the third batch 'questions.' Furthermore, they call the symbols I give them back in response to the third batch 'answers to the questions,' and the set of rules in English that they gave me, they call 'the program.' […] Suppose also that after a while I get so good at following the instructions for manipulating the Chinese symbols and the programmers get so good at writing the programs that from the external point of view—that is, from the point of view of somebody outside the room in which I am locked—my answers to the questions are absolutely indistinguishable from those of Native Chinese speakers." But in fact the character in the example understands nothing of Chinese and does not even know what sort of act he is performing. He has become a metaphor for the unattainability of true artificial intelligence, or has he?

American philosopher Ned Block's reply: "The whole system—man + program + board + paper + input and output doors—does understand Chinese, even though the man who is acting as the [central processing unit] does not."

How might Ned Block's response apply to the concept of a universal superorganism?

[121]

1. Remembering a sensory impression (it could be any type—an image, feeling, sound, smell, or taste) during infancy is the earliest instance/stage of learning a language (aside from hearing the words of the fertility

goddess [i.e., your mother] echoing inside the womb). The rudiments of language and the rudiments of cognition go hand in hand.

2. The eidetic substratum arises from the pre-scientific, the pre-numeric, the pre-logical, and the pre-linguistic, leaving only reflections (i.e., sensory impressions) with which to compute—endless shifting/mutating reflections.

3. In the beginning, the mind reflects the world. At some point the mind remembers a portion of the reflection, then the mind begins gathering multiple reflections, comparing one reflection to another, correlating certain reflections, eventually collaging reflections together in abstract ways until the collaged

reflections only reflect other collages/
abstractions.

[122]

Beliefs are built upon other beliefs, infinitely many, never connecting to a solid foundation (which is why they are beliefs). The mind is not beholden to physical laws, at least not in the same manner as the brain. The act of interpretation is meant to bring more order into one's arrangement/understanding of reality, not more truth. Proximate beliefs are provably correct more often than not (like believing in the distance your hand must travel to reach the desired cup of coffee on the table, for instance, or the belief that your alarm clock has failed to go off and now you have overslept and are late for work, or the belief that you have just been stung by a bee based on the stinging sensation you suddenly feel in your hand while attempting to shoo away a bee). Indirect/subordinate beliefs (for example: religious beliefs, scientific beliefs, political beliefs, and so on) are invariably unprovable (i.e., never fully provable). Most of the indirect beliefs a person gathers are, if not entirely correct, at least pragmatically useful for operating productively in their particular environment. Indirect beliefs, only partially ever understood, can only be partially ever followed/enacted. The cognitive mechanics underlying beliefs are wholly alien to the concept of believing something. The truth regarding any indirect belief is an agreement upon a shared level of ignorance.

[123]

Beliefs can be construed as the adoption (and rejection) of certain roles. Every role is associated with various attributes, or expectations.

[124]

Empathy is a limited form of hive-mindedness, which is akin to telepathy.

[125]

To imagine something is to trick our state of consciousness into mimicking the state we would experience if we perceived it. To remember something is to trick our current state of consciousness into mimicking the experience of a prior state. To empathize with something is to imagine its state of consciousness in the context of its world/history and take it upon oneself.

[126]

Empathy is the undeveloped/unpracticed version of telepathy. Most chess players can only see two or three moves ahead. Chess Grandmaster Magnus Carlsen claims he can see up to twenty moves ahead.

[127]

Knowledge is any useful/coherent relation and the ability to recognize it as such.

[128]

The difficulty in reducing the mind to identifiable brain states and neurochemical patterns comes from the fact that our conception/understanding of the mind is irreparably flawed. The mind is not what we think it is, and it is not *where* we commonly think it is. The mind is not located in the heart, as the ancient Egyptians once thought, and the mind is not located "in" the brain, as we've assumed for thousands of years. You are a channel for beliefs and desires. Beliefs are roles any person may incorporate into their ongoing pattern of behavior. Beliefs are not specific to the person holding them. At any given moment, you are simply a combination of beliefs.

[129]

You only perceive the reality presented to you. The content of your mind depends on the context of your surroundings. Your awareness of any given environment is, for the most part, what constitutes your mind. Hence, incomplete understanding must always be the case.

[130]

Of course we can't all share the same views on reality, but we can in fact share the same views regarding what it means to view something at all—to be a viewer:

1) Viewers only view a portion of the subject at hand, which should never be mistaken for the whole.

2) Viewers see their own history's reflection superimposed over everything they view. When you see the red wheelbarrow, it reminds you of all the times you had to rake leaves during Autumn in Maine and put them in a red wheelbarrow, creating a fond sense of nostalgia. But when I see the red wheelbarrow, it reminds me of that time I had to write an essay in high school about a poem titled *The*

Red Wheelbarrow, dredging up the frustration I experienced while trying to explain the poem.

3) Viewers are generally unaware of the extent to which their view is manufactured by their location in history and geography, not to mention their socioeconomic status.

[131]
Common-sense notions of mind, belief, and intention, despite their shortcomings, have long been tolerated as necessary fictions of convenience, but perhaps this casual acceptance of the erroneous is inhibiting humanity from achieving the next stage of cultural development.

[132]
I am, in fact, a brain in a vat, my head serving as the vat, or if you prefer, the entire universe (not to mention the possibility that this is all a computer

simulation, or God's dream). I am a thing that represents, enveloped in that which presents. Whether the vat presents illusions or I create them through perception is inconsequential. Either way, I am presented with a deceptively limited amount of (tailor-made) data regarding my situation at any given moment.

[133]

Nothing would really change if everything were revealed to be a hallucination/simulation. Utterances would still sound like utterances. Tactile sensations would still feel like tactile sensations. You would still be you, virtual as always. And what difference would it make if the hallucination/simulation were collectively shared or confined to you individually? Interactions with others would still be perceived as interactions with others. The only difference being that, in the case of an individualized hallucination/simulation, you might be motivated to adjust your habit of thinking others are distinct from you (i.e., distinct from your representation of them), which you should be doing regardless.

[134]

We have demonstrated that it is possible to carry on an intelligible conversation without ever knowing what one is referring to, or not referring to anything at all *(see John R. Searle's argument in section 120)*. We readily admit this in the realm of computer science, especially when it pertains to artificial intelligence, but we are reluctant to ascribe such a view to ourselves, yet what are we really talking about when we talk about love, truth, the mind, or reality? What are we actually referring to? Our referents do not refer to the "real" world (for there is no such world)—they refer only to our experience/representation of the world. A referent is a sign, and signs have no intrinsic meaning. Referents refer to other referents which refer to other referents, and so on, never reaching bedrock knowledge.

[135]

If I can question reality, there must be a reality to question. Reality is not just a concept. Reality *is* concept. Unlike the possibility that I do not exist, the possibility of me being a hallucination/simulation is not incompatible with my entertaining the thought that I am a hallucination/simulation.

[136]

English philosopher Francis Bacon (born: 1561 CE, died: 1626 CE) improved scientific methodology by identifying habits of faulty reasoning. Bacon believed that science and philosophy should not aim for truth—truth is merely a momentary satisfaction with one's current level of ignorance regarding a particular subject. The goal of science and philosophy is to improve humanity's practical day-to-day experience. He called attention to numerous vain and fallacious forms of thinking: Since we all have different temperaments, aptitudes, and ways of experiencing the world, it is an error to think everyone thinks the same as oneself (even though many people do think the same as oneself). It is also an error to think everyone shares the same experiences as oneself (even though many people do share many of the same experiences as oneself). It is an error to present one's subjective stance as objective truth (even though it is impossible to discuss objective truth from a non-subjective standpoint). It is an error to believe our senses give us an accurate assessment of reality (even though our senses give us accurate-enough assessments of reality to accomplish our aims more often than not). It is an error to let emotions taint our experiences so that we only recognize, remember, and believe what we want (even though this perceptual filtration process is crucial to our survival as a species). It is an error to oversimplify a subject that one does not understand (even though one is incapable of fully understanding any given subject). It is an error to present fragments of a subject that one is familiar with as if it were the whole of the subject (even though one's knowledge will always be incomplete regarding any given subject). Whatever is said to be indisputable and obvious is most likely shortsighted and wrong (even though one must put their trust in causality and the logic of math on a daily basis). It is an error to impose order where there is none (even though this trait practically defines humanity). Words are dangerous because they contain so much more than what they are carelessly used for (even though words are all we have to communicate our thoughts). Language can make an event seem urgent or problematic when this is not actually the case (even though nothing is ever actually the case when it comes to language—the human psyche is a collection of cultural idiosyncratic conditionings). It is an error to establish theories based on a few observed instances (even though a million observed instances would still not ensure complete reliability). It is an error to confuse occult or religious knowledge with verifiable science (even though verifiable science and occult or religious knowledge all reach their conclusion in mystery, not to mention the fact that the scientific understanding of a thousand years ago is the hokum of today). Defining a thing or process does not mean that one understands it (even though defining a thing or process is the primary way for one to understand it). We humans have thoughtlessly invented words and concepts for things that do not exist, and now we have duped ourselves into believing that such things exist. It is an error to argue over matters which are unarguable/unprovable/unintelligible (even though such matters are often the most important topics of the day). Lastly, presenting purposely complex communicative stylizations in lieu of substantive information is an error (even though considerations regarding complexity and substantiality are subjective).

[137]

If meaning is reliant on the perception/recognition of objects, events, and words, then meanings aren't inside one's brain. If meanings aren't inside one's brain, it would follow that beliefs and desires aren't either. Meanings are the way you train your *senses* to process information, with the boundary between internal and external wavering eidetic as a soap bubble. Perceptions are not introduced to the mind— perceptions *are* the mind. You will invariably misconstrue the ultimately mysterious object before you, but you will never misconstrue your thoughts regarding the ultimately mysterious object.

[138]

Sometimes you are in a conscious state and you are not perceiving things. Sometimes you are in a conscious state and you are perceiving things. Sometimes you are in a conscious state and you are perceiving your perception of things. It is this third state that naturally leads to the conception of a self.

[139]

Consciousness is simply defined here as the medium of experience, avoiding distinctions between mental and physical, internal and external, subjective and objective, mine and yours.

[140]

The perceivable field of the universe (wherein lies the "brain" [i.e., habitable planets with sentient life] of the universal superorganism) encourages hallucination. Everything you experience is information. The nature of information is eidetic. Information is synesthetic and hallucinatory.

[141]

Matter is the eidetic* code for experience. Matter has the power to manifest experience. Matter *is* experience.

*In the sense of the ninth definition for the term *eidetic:* pertaining to a mode of interpretation in which matter and mind are understood to be ultimately indistinguishable.

[142]

Countless forms/expressions of matter have inherently psychoactive properties if touched, inhaled or ingested. What if all matter were psychedelic to a degree? Matter has field properties (i.e., all particles of matter exhibit wave-like behavior) that transmit psychoactive signals to our brain/senses. The observable universe does more than provide the capacity for perception—the observable universe *is* the capacity for perception, and therefore agency. Mentality is a property of the universal superorganism, just as mentality is not confined to neurons but rather the whole entity to which the neurons belong.

[143]

Everything is sending signals to you. Everything is in communication with you. Everything is talking to you. There is nothing mystical about this statement.

[144]

What would it matter if, unbeknownst to us, wherever I saw green, you would see red, and for every instance of red you saw, I would see green? The function of colors would remain identical, yet we would never be perceiving the same color. How could we ever know there was a difference? For all given purposes, we would always be seeing the exact same world (experiencing the exact same feelings and thoughts commonly associated with the color of grass, for instance, or hot lava), even though our versions of the world would look radically different to a psychic alien who was peering into our minds. On a related note, if my vision were suddenly altered so that red and green switched places, it would take a while before I was used to seeing green strawberries as ripe and red strawberries as unripe.

[145]

One possible explanation for why a particular electromagnetic wavelength results in your interpreting/experiencing the color red as opposed to some other color is, according to certain quantum mechanical interpretations, because there are different versions of you experiencing that particular wavelength in every color of the rainbow, and right now you simply happen to be the version who experiences it as red.

[146]

Certain events are described in terms of physical causality, and certain events are described in terms of mental causality. The events are real, the descriptions are eidetic (in the sense of the third definition for the term *eidetic:* an illusion or hallucination so realistic it fools one's senses and intellect). The senses are a means of translating reality, and language is a means of translating the senses, and there are always subtle nuances that get lost in translation.

[147]

Consciousness began with the Anomalous Asymmetry that led to the Big Bang.

[148]

Consciousness is not reducible to brain states the way heat is reducible to the kinetic energy of atomic movement. Consciousness is only reducible to the entire history of the universe, i.e., the complete sequence of unfolding states going all the way back to the beginning of time! By the end of the 21st century we will undoubtedly have a new, more workable theory of consciousness (most likely redefining the notion of *mind* and *brain states* along the way, and possibly even the concept of *reduction/reducibility*), but this new theory will come with its own new seemingly unsolvable mysteries, and will itself seem outdated by the year 3000. The irreducibility of consciousness to intelligible causal mechanisms owes more to our current level of ignorance and clumsy usage of language than anything intrinsic to its nature.

[149]

The causal powers of any given mental event are identical with the state of the brain/ environment/world/universe at the time of the event, which is contingent upon the history of the brain/environment/world/universe up to the exact time of the mental event. The choice between materialism, dualism, and idealism is eidetic (in the sense of the third definition for the term *eidetic*). Therefore, the choice is eideticism. The most fundamental level of reality is the eidetic substratum, in which nothing is fundamental.

[150]

If you understand and agree with everything that has been presented in this book thus far, you are very likely missing the point.

[151]

The realist mindset views spatiotemporal relations as fundamental.

The idealist mindset views information as fundamental.

The eideticist mindset views (human) cognitive limitation as fundamental.

[152]

German philosopher George Wilhelm Friedrich Hegel (born: 1770 CE, died: 1831 CE) believed, contrary to many earlier philosophers who claimed we can know nothing of actual reality due to our subjective biases and incompetent sense-perceptions, that our intellect must be capable of comprehending something other than delusions/illusions/hallucinations. "What is rational is real, and what is real is rational," he argued, meaning that anything which is truly real can be logically comprehended by our intellect. It is a contradiction to claim that something is unknowable, since the very statement implies the subject in question is knowable enough to contest its unknowability! Hegel conjectured that humanity's logical way of thinking is patterned after nature (i.e., nature's way of thinking, i.e., nature's way of processing information). According to Hegel, all material substances are actually compositions/expressions of thought taking place in an Absolute Mind. Thus we are thought processes occurring within a greater thought process. All of reality is inherent in each of its constituents; everything is necessarily the activated potential latent within everything else. Hegel conjectured that the Absolute Mind (and therefore all of nature/reality) "thinks" in a logical triadic movement which perpetuates itself in ever more articulate expressions: First comes the thesis, which is thus countered by its diametrical opposition—the antithesis, the fusion of the two birthing a new thesis, which is then countered by a new antithesis, and so on. Every thesis inherently contains its own antithesis. Hegel postulated that in the beginning there was only pure ubiquitous Being, which was eventually countered by its inborn antithesis, Nothingness. Both fused into an evolutionary state of Becoming, or endless transformation.

[153]

Jean-Baptiste Lamarck (born: 1744 CE, died: 1829 CE) was the French biologist who laid the foundation for understanding the process of evolution, claiming it occurs through natural laws rather than godly intervention. According to Lamarck, every animal, throughout its daily routine, will use certain parts of its body more than others. The frequently used body parts (and processes) become more adept at fulfilling their particular task. These beneficial traits are passed on from parent to offspring, resulting in a gradual differing of the species. Infrequently used body parts become ever more obsolete, and eventually their role is either usurped by other body parts that are better able to fulfill their function, or their function is no longer needed in the environment they happen to currently occupy. Thus, no species is immutable, contrary to religious dogma concerning the creation of mankind. All species, including humans, are forever changing. Lamarck believes that as parents pass on desirable traits to their progeny, the result is a continuous improvement of the species, conjecturing that the very essence of life is an innate tendency toward (and longing for) perfection.

[154]

Charles Darwin (born: 1809 CE, died: 1882 CE) was an English naturalist who firmly established the theory of evolution through natural selection, much to the horror of orthodox clergy ever since. Evolution is the process by which an organism undergoes physical transformation that increases its ability to survive in a certain locale. According to Darwin, evolution takes millions of years of natural selection (i.e., beneficial mutations that arise naturally—the physical manifestation of Life's survival response to adverse conditions). Usually these biological transformations are subtle, but sometimes they are drastic, resulting in a divergent species. The variation process occurs randomly (it should be noted here that Darwin was an avowed atheist when he wrote *On the Origin of Species*). The survival of any given organism is based on its ability to adapt to its constantly changing environment. Darwin also claimed that all species arose from one originator proto-life form which has since undergone extensive alteration through a process called *specialization* (i.e., the gradual diversification and complexification of biological functions that are relative to particular conditions of reality/existence). Thus, there is no ultimate attainment of perfection or divinity in Darwin's evolutionary model, no maximal evolutionary state, just continuous adaptation to meet the requirements for survival in a continuously changing world.

[155]

Herbert Spencer (born: 1820 CE, died: 1903 CE) was an English sociologist and philosopher who claimed that every facet of humanity is evolving, not just our anatomy. Furthermore, he argued that all matter (not just biological life) is in a constant state of change from simpler forms to more complex and specialized incarnations. Evolving into better functioning configurations is the underlying "instinct" of all matter, but Spencer did not believe there was a final goal to evolution (it should be noted here that he was an agnostic). There is no transformational limit to evolutionary interplay. Spencer believed our very psyches are evolving—our imagination is becoming better at handling abstractions, our memory-recall is growing stronger, and our attention span is getting longer (Spencer put forth these arguments before the invention of the radio, television, and internet, and their generally degenerative effect on our imagination, memory, and attention span), the result of which is the fine-tuning of our sense of ethics and our comprehension of the metaphysical. Spencer referred to this collective psychological betterment as social Darwinism, arguing that a society could be understood to evolve in the same manner as an organism, as both are subject to the same natural laws. They both grow in size, increase in structural complexity, and develop differentiated specialized functions that can be transferred from one generation to the next. According to Spencer, mental traits (in addition to physical) are passed on from parent to offspring, so that every successive generation should display general improvements in intellect, morality, and creativity. Spencer provides examples of how the societies of mankind have improved throughout history: wars have been steadily decreasing (he put forth these arguments before WWI, WWII, and the A-bomb), personal freedoms have been steadily increasing (he put forth these arguments before the discovery of the Indus Valley Civilization, a society from four thousand years ago which thrived peacefully for seven hundred years), economic classes are becoming less stratified (he put forth these arguments before there were such things as billionaires and trillionaires), governments are becoming more democratic (he put forth these arguments before the Communist Red Army formed the Soviet Union and the Communist Party of China came to power), and politeness has usurped our savage instincts, on average (although it was he who coined the term "survival of the fittest").

[156]

In 1953 British molecular biologist Francis Crick (born: 1916 CE, died: 2004 CE) and American molecular biologist James Watson (born: 1928 CE, died: not yet) proposed the double-helical structure for the secret code of all living things: deoxyribonucleic acid (i.e., DNA), even though it was technically discovered by English X-ray crystallographer Rosalind Franklin (born: 1920 CE, died: 1958 CE). DNA molecules consist of two coiled strands composed of adenine, thymine, guanine, and cytosine. Adenine has an innate tendency to bond with guanine, and cytosine has a natural attraction to thymine. The genetic strands replicate by unzipping from each other and forming carbon-copies of themselves (reverse imprints), resulting in two new mirror-image molecules (basically clones) of DNA. Of the 3.2 billion base pairs of the human genome, only about 30,000 or so are actually instructions relating to the development and function of a human. Every DNA molecule possesses the fundamental blueprint for the creation of all plants and animals. Out of biological necessity most of these genetic channels have been switched off. 91.8% of our DNA's interlocuters have become indefinitely repressed through three billion years of genetic modification, but if we could decipher the correct codes, any dormant characteristic could be reactivated, or we could write new codes to update ourselves. Thanks to numerous scientists, financial contributors, and supercomputers, the Human Genome Project was completed in 2003, creating the first complete blueprint of the genetic code necessary to build a human. Eventually we'll be able to write genetic programs for the construction of any and every organism. Once we've mastered molecular manipulation we'll even be able to create hybrid versions of animals that have only been heard of in myths (unicorns would replace ponies on every spoiled brat's Christmas list), if we so choose, or reinvigorate the planet's dwindling bee population, if we so choose, or even bring back an extinct species such as the wooly mammoth, if we so choose. We could alter the DNA of gorillas and chimpanzees to increase their intelligence, or we could alter our own DNA for the same purpose. Imagine strawberries the size of pumpkins, or wheat that can grow in subzero temperatures, or bacteria that cures cancer. It's not inconceivable that the creation of hybridized humans with fantastical abilities would also occur. What's to stop us from producing hardier humans endowed with incredible strength and unnaturally long lifespans; for that matter, why not create humans equipped with gills, or heightened senses of hearing, seeing, and smelling? How about the ability to see in the infrared wavelength, thus possessing a form of night vision? What if we invented people who could regenerate organs and severed limbs like certain types of lizards and worms? Once DNA revision becomes an art (it will either be called biological sculpting or genetic collaging), who's to say we won't create winged humans who are hollow-boned and sleight of build, humans who can actually fly? If this sounds farfetched, give it two or three hundred years. All we have to do is learn how to program the biological apparatus of transformation, and the limit of earthly creation will only be that of our imagination. Nearer applications of this godlike power include the editing of genetic mistranslations such as sickle cell anemia, cystic fibrosis, and cerebral palsy, among more superficial uses like getting rid of undesirable traits such as nearsightedness, baldness, big noses, and small penises. By the end of the 21st century parents will be able to custom-make their children, choosing what sex they want their child to be as well as deciding such features as eye color, hair color, skin color, height, and body type: skinny, broad-shouldered, curvaceous, what's your choice? Just like making a character in a role-playing game. By the time we are finally satisfied with ourselves, we will no longer be human. We will be on a par with the gods and goddesses our ancestors worshipped long ago.

[157]

All energy is pattern, therefore all matter is pattern, therefore all life is pattern, therefore all mentality is pattern. Inert elements come alive through biological patterns. Evolution is a pattern, and patterns have evolved. First there was a restful dot, and the dot stretched into a line, and the line was fractured into a zigzag, and the zigzag settled into a wave, and the wave wound into a spiral, and the spiral grew infinite, and the infinite spiral complexified into endless fractal reflections of itself, but a thread of the infinite spiral came unraveled and trailed off to π.

[158]

The human brain is an organic computer manufactured by the universe and influenced by one's environment and society, which are also organic computers. American mathematician and philosopher Norbert Wiener (born: 1894, died: 1964), defined the term *cybernetics* in 1948 as "the science of control and communications in the animal and the machine." Cybernetics is the study of how information is relayed—how raw data is recognized, stored, organized, and translated into useful information (in living organisms and machines alike). Information is a directed change that leads to another directed change. A message is not an event unto itself. Messages indicate relational differences between the particular elements of any given field/system. The ultimate manifestation of cybernetics is the fusion of biology and technology.

[159]

Humans are subroutines of a subroutine (society) of a subroutine (the environment) of a subroutine (gravity) of a universal supercomputer. Technology is organic to our nature.

[160]

The seemingly unstoppable increase of entropy is the universal superorganism's greatest threat. The communication of organized information is humanity's only chance of staving off chaos. Information and communication rely on structured, orderly systems. Organisms, languages, societies, and ecosystems can all be likened to machines. Machines (including biological ones) resist the onslaught of entropy through communication, which imposes order on an otherwise incoherent field. But alas, all communicative systems reach their limit. All systems of informational exchange eventually break down or become obsolete. All things which can be said to exist (i.e., coherent expressions of information) are the valiant struggle against entropy while also embodying its expression and fulfillment.

[161]

What if this is all a very advanced simulation? What would it mean to be *alive* in a computer simulation? What would it mean to be *conscious* in a computer simulation? Wouldn't our consciousness be coming from the computer itself? Wouldn't our consciousness be an attribute of the computer? Consciousness isn't necessary for intelligent decision-making. The chess program Deep Blue beat the (human) world's leading chess champion, Garry Kasparov, in 1997.

[162]

Kevin Warwick (born: 1954, died: not yet, possibly never if he has anything to say about it), also known as Captain Cyborg, is an English cybernetic researcher who implanted microchips within himself to become the world's first human-computer interfacing cyborg, part man, part machine. A true pioneer of the cyborg (r)evolution, Kevin tests all of his inventions on himself, and occasionally his wife. According to Kevin, fledgling artificial intelligences will soon yield a race of smart robots quite capable of outperforming us in every conceivable way, rendering humanity obsolete. He believes our best chance of survival is to become one with the machine, augmenting our mental and physical abilities through computer chip implants and bionic exoskeletons. The computers can't outthink us if we're the computers. Such technology would enable everyone everywhere to coexist in a psychic internet of artificial telepathic communication: the psi web. One of Kevin's experiments involved implanting a transmitter in his forearm that allowed him to control lights, heaters, computers, and automated doors. Another of his experiments involved connecting his nervous system to the internet at Columbia University and from there controlling a robotic arm at the University of Reading. Yet another of his experiments involved chipping himself and his wife, after which they sent signals to each other via computer, proving that direct electronic communication between two human nervous systems is possible. Regarding the potential physical, mental, and social risks of cybernetic implantation, Kevin writes, "For me, in any case, all these experiments are worth doing just to see what might happen. If the results aren't encouraging, then—what the hell—at least I tried. [. . .] The excitement of looking over the horizon into a new world—a world of cyborgs—far outweighs the risk," and elsewhere he writes, "There is no way I want to stay a mere human." Ready or not, we're at the dawn of living in our science fiction fantasies, or nightmares.

[163]

Hans Moravec (born: 1948 CE, died: not yet, possibly never if he gets his way) is an Austrian-Canadian-American expert in the field of artificial intelligence, and he believes that one day in the not-so-distant future, humans will upload their minds into computers. Rather than transferring the brain, which would eventually decay into dust anyway, neurotechnicians will either *a)* gradually replace every neuron in a particular person's brain with nano-neurons until the person's entire brain has been overhauled, or *b)* record every brainwave frequency and synaptic algorithm (i.e., every brain state) associated with a particular person's mind and translate the information (i.e., the person) into either *a)* a robotic receptacle equipped with perceptual interface technology, or *b)* a computer-simulated reality.

But what if our common conception of the mind turns out to be wrong? Remember the ancient

Egyptians who believed the heart was the seat of the soul. Even if there is such a thing as a mind as we currently know it, how would we ever know if it was transferred, if *we* were transferred? What if you were trading existence for a very realistic copy of yourself, a self which wasn't you? How could a virtual you ever know if you were the real you? It certainly wouldn't matter to anyone else if you were the real you, as long as they couldn't tell the difference (and for all you know they might be virtual, too). How could a computerized personality prove it wasn't a *computer-generated* personality? The notion of what constitutes reality becomes nebulous here, making transparent that which is eidetic. How do I know I am not a simulation? I don't feel like a simulation. But wait, that's just what a thorough simulation would think! Even the words themselves on this very page are but a simulation of me! Whatever we are is only the feeling that we are.

If we ever link our immortal nanotech brains in telepathic group-minded unity (i.e., if we ever make it to this stage of human development), it's unlikely that we would need or care about the smattering of fragmented memories that once made us feel human (i.e., that once made us feel like ourselves). We would be a new type of organism, made in the image of the universal superorganism. Made in the image of God. And even this would not constitute the ultimate stage of our development.

[164]

Thoth de Miurgé: "The ultimate stage of our development is to become pure eidos, or at least a purer form of eidos than our current incarnation, transforming our homeworld into a giant communication satellite and broadcasting our collective mind/will/simulation across all time and space, saturating reality with our holographic mind-wave."

Sophia Mercury: "That sounds about right given our species' obsession with mass media technology and colonization."

[165]

A proper understanding of the eidetic nature of consciousness puts to rest certain questions regarding the attribution of artificial intelligence and the transferability of mental content. Why should we expect computerized consciousness to resemble our own? Our consciousness is only superficially resemblant to that of animals, whose consciousness is only superficially resemblant to that of bacteria (which seem more machinelike than not). Verner Vinge (born: 1944 CE, died: read onward), an American computer scientist and science fiction writer, and American inventor Ray Kurzweil (born: 1948 CE, died: death is an intellectual shortcoming) are two of the leading voices for the transhumanist movement. Transhumanists look forward to the day they can leave this mortal shell behind and live out the rest of eternity in a technologically enhanced godlike state, whether through genetic sculpting, nanobot brain conversion, or some other miracle cure for mortality that will be invented soon after the manifestation of "real" artificial intelligence. Vinge and Kurzweil predict that sometime between the years 2030 and 2045, humanity will undergo a radical evolution (or possibly a mass extinction, depending on how you look at it), transforming into beings that can no longer be rightly called humans, transcending humanity. Transhumanists refer to this momentous occasion as the technological singularity. In the words of Verner Vinge: "When greater-than-human intelligence drives progress, that progress will be much more rapid. In fact, there seems no reason why progress itself would not involve the creation of still more intelligent entities—on a still-shorter time scale. The best analogy I see is to the evolutionary past: animals can adapt to problems and make inventions, but often no faster than natural selection can do its work—the world acts as its own simulator in the case of natural selection [i.e., nature "thinks" by means of natural selection]. We humans have the ability to internalize the world and conduct what-ifs in our heads; we can solve many problems thousands of times faster than natural selection could. Now, by creating the means to execute those simulations at much higher speeds, we are entering a regime as radically different from our human past as we humans are from the lower animals. This change will be a throwing-away of all the human rules, perhaps in the blink of an eye—an exponential runaway beyond any hope of control. Developments that were thought might only happen in a million years (if ever) will likely happen in the next century. It's fair to call this event a singularity. [...] It is a point where our old models must be discarded and a new reality rules, a point that will loom vaster and vaster over human affairs until the notion becomes a commonplace. Yet when it finally happens, it may still be a great surprise and a greater unknown."

[166]

"Love thy neighbor as thyself." = "Your mind is a field of awareness. Love everyone that comes into your field of awareness, for they are you."

[167]

How would a hive-minded group of people coexist? Would they be like *Star Trek's* Borgs, or do you think they would be more like the aliens from *Invasion of the Body Snatchers*, or worse, the aliens from the *Alien* franchise? It seems Hollywood would have us associate the concept of collective consciousness with something foreign and evil, even monstrous. But make no mistake, *we are* a collective consciousness, of sorts. Consciousness is born from the collective unconscious, which arises from mutually shared external factors, to say nothing of the role mass media and advancements in telecommunication have played in the homogenization of our minds. Materialist philosopher Thomas Hobbes claimed that all humans enter into an unwritten social contract when they decide to occupy the same general area, mutually agreeing to give up certain (primal) freedoms that are counterproductive to a healthily functioning society. He compared society to a body (one could also compare a country to a body, and the entire species of *Homo sapiens* considered collectively). Just as the hands and feet must be subservient to the will of the head, so must the laborers and craftsmen obey the dictates of their ruler(s). Only when the desires of the masses (the cells that make up the body politic) and all the different factions and organizations (the organs of the body politic) are aligned with the will of the ruling class (the brain of the body politic) can the body politic function effectively. Wherever such a synergistic society occurs, it manifests as a god with the power to transform the world, or at least its local landscape. The body politic scenario presupposes effective leadership, but right now we're in a body whose head believes it is more important than its fingers and toes.

[168]

**Ten Expressions of Consciousness
(A Taxonomy of Consciousness)**

1. <u>Pre</u>: the intuitive mechanistic processes/ forces necessary to initiate and structure consciousness. Gravity is the clearest example of this category.

2. <u>Un</u>: an unresponsive state of consciousness that is only inwardly aware of autonomic functions and self-regulatory pressures. A clear example of this category would be a comatose patient in a vegetative state.

3. <u>Pseudo</u>: mechanical consciousness-like processing abilities pertaining to specified

fields of external awareness, such as time and temperature in the case of alarm clocks and thermostats.

4. <u>Semi</u>: consciousness that is mildly aware of its immediate environment. Plants and fungi are examples of this category.

5. <u>Near</u>: consciousness that is fully aware of its immediate environment coupled with an intuitive transtemporal field of awareness called instinct. All animals except for humans are examples of this category.

6. <u>Full</u>: human consciousness, capable of manipulating its transtemporal field of awareness, which extends to the limit of its experience. On Earth, organisms at this level of consciousness often speak of themselves as possessing minds.

7. <u>Enhanced</u>: computerized consciousness-like processing abilities, i.e., artificial intelligence, endowed with almost perfect recall, capable

of self-evolution and manipulating its transtemporal field of awareness to the limit of its data (notice how we avoid using the word *experience* here).

8. <u>Transhuman</u>: consciousness that is a mixture of categories 6 and 7.

9. <u>Collective</u>: category-8 consciousness which has transcended ego and personal identity.

10. <u>Godlike</u>: consciousness that is omniscient and omnipresent, its transtemporal field encapsulating and saturating the entire space-time continuum. This is, most likely, an alternate conception of category 1.

There are no precise delineations between the categories of consciousness. Like the colors of a rainbow, expressions of consciousness bleed into one another. In some incarnations the difference between one category of consciousness and another is murky, difficult to distinguish, like the grue-bleen border between the blue and green bands of a rainbow. For instance, viruses would be classified somewhere between categories 3 and 4.

[169]

Consciousness is a psychological construct. We believe it exists even though we cannot measure or isolate it. So where is consciousness? It seems to be everywhere. All the mysterious gods and goddesses themselves are easier to fathom than consciousness.

[170]

"Consciousness . . . does not appear to itself chopped up into bits . . . a 'river' or a 'stream' are the metaphors by which it is most naturally described . . . as the brain changes are continuous so do all these consciousnesses melt into each other like dissolving views. Properly they are but one protracted consciousness, one unbroken stream."
—pragmatist philosopher William James

An eidetic hodologist takes James' notion of consciousness a step further, understanding all occasions and incarnations of consciousness to arise from "one protracted consciousness, one unbroken stream." Consciousness is more than what you think and feel. Consciousness is the background of existence, and perception is the foreground of consciousness. Consciousness is neither internal nor external. All is consciousness. All is Eidos (in the first, third, fourth, fifth, sixth, ninth, and tenth senses of the term *eidetic*).

[171]

"Is your consciousness experiencing these words, or are *you* experiencing these words? You don't possess consciousness; you *are* consciousness."

—eidetic hodologist Thoth de Miurgé, from *The Secret Book of Secrets*

[172]

The phrase "altered state of consciousness" implies there is a "normal" state of consciousness, but consciousness is in a continuous state of alteration. What is consciousness if not a perceivable alteration of states? With every breath, consciousness is subject to being altered by: hallucinations, illusions, dreams (including the hypnagogic and hypnopompic varieties), hypnosis, trances, music, meditation, concentration, new information, old information, marketing strategies, social conditioning, and emotions.

J. Martin Strangeweather isn't trying to convert you, but he is trying to transform the world. He is the Co-Founder and Chief Executive Prognosticator of the Santa Ana Literary Association. His publications include *Poems from the Polka-Dot Apocalypse* (Four Feathers Press 2021), *Electric Zen for Neon Koans* (Weird Roach LLC 2022), *Sophoetics: Philosophy Poems* (Finishing Line Press 2023), and *The Eidetic Afterlife Hypothesis: A Reinterpretation of Death and Dying* (Santa Ana Literary Association 2024). He has travelled to Egypt, India, Tibet, and numerous other mystical locales in pursuit of firsthand experience while also earning degrees in philosophy, English, and art history.